The History of the Island of Dominica.

Thomas Atwood, J. Johnson

Copyright © BiblioLife, LLC

This book represents a historical reproduction of a work originally published before 1923 that is part of a unique project which provides opportunities for readers, educators and researchers by bringing hard-to-find original publications back into print at reasonable prices. Because this and other works are culturally important, we have made them available as part of our commitment to protecting, preserving and promoting the world's literature. These books are in the "public domain" and were digitized and made available in cooperation with libraries, archives, and open source initiatives around the world dedicated to this important mission.

We believe that when we undertake the difficult task of re-creating these works as attractive, readable and affordable books, we further the goal of sharing these works with a global audience, and preserving a vanishing wealth of human knowledge.

Many historical books were originally published in small fonts, which can make them very difficult to read. Accordingly, in order to improve the reading experience of these books, we have created "enlarged print" versions of our books. Because of font size variation in the original books, some of these may not technically qualify as "large print" books, as that term is generally defined; however, we believe these versions provide an overall improved reading experience for many.

THE HISTORY OF THE ISLAND OF DOMINICA.

CONTAINING

A DESCRIPTION OF ITS SITUATION, EXTENT, CLIMATE, MOUNTAINS, RIVERS, NATURAL PRODUCTIONS, &c. &c.

TOGETHER WITH

AN ACCOUNT OF THE CIVIL GOVERNMENT, TRADE, LAWS, CUSTOMS, AND MANNERS OF THE DIFFERENT INHABITANTS OF THAT ISLAND. ITS CONQUEST BY THE FRENCH, AND RESTORATION TO THE BRITISH DOMINIONS.

By THOMAS ATWOOD.

LONDON:

PRINTED FOR J. JOHNSON, NO. 72, ST. PAUL'S CHURCH-YARD.

M DCC XCI.

INTRODUCTION.

IT is greatly to be lamented, that although the island of Dominica is so very capable of being rendered one of the chief, if not the best, the English have in the West Indies; yet, from a want of knowledge of its importance, or inattention, it is at this time almost as much unsettled, as when it was ceded to Great Britain, near thirty years ago.

This is the more remarkable, from the great consequence the possession of it is to the English, in case of a rupture with France, it being the key of the British dominions in that part of the world, and from its situation between the two principal settlements of the French, Martinique and Guadeloupe, it is the only place in the West Indies, by which there is a possibility for Great Britain to maintain the sovereignty of those seas.

It has moreover many conveniences for the service of both an army and fleet, which few other West India islands can boast; and was it to be well settled with British subjects, would be of material assistance to our other possessions, by furnishing them with many articles of which they very often are greatly in need.

For the purpose of bringing forth to view these capabilities of Dominica, the following history of that island is submitted to the candid perusal of a generous public by the author; whose chief inducement for writing it, was his hope, that it might be some small means of service to a country, in which he has spent several years of his life, and the prosperity of which, it is his ardent wish to see speedily promoted.

The history of distant settlements belonging to Great Britain, it is presumed, cannot fail of being acceptable to every Englishman who wishes well to his country; and however deficient this essay of his may be, in point of erudition, correctness, or correspondent circumstances, yet, from its being the

first

first on the subject, the author hopes it may meet with a favourable reception.

It falls not within the compass of this work to enter into details of acts of the legislature, the conduct of governors, or of individuals of that island; these he leaves for a more extensive work, or for abler pens to record; and if what is here submitted to public perusal serve in the least to promote the welfare of the present and future inhabitants of Dominica, and thereby the interests of the British nation at large, the purpose of the author by this publication will be fully answered.

London, May 1791.

CONTENTS.

CHAP. I.

Description of the island, its situation, extent, climate, and other subjects; together with an account of the conquest of it, its cession to Great Britain, and the disposal of the lands by the crown.   Page 1

CHAP. II.

Description of the soil, mountains, and woods; of valuable timber, and other trees; also of the birds of the woods peculiar to the island.   17

CHAP. III.

Of the rivers and lakes in the island, river and fresh water fish, also of sea fish, land crabs, and a description of the native quadruped, and other animals.   35

CHAP. IV.

Of the most remarkable reptiles and insects of the island, their venomous and other qualities, with remarks.   51

CHAP. V.

An account of the different articles of West India produce raised in the island; the number of sugar and coffee plantations therein, with remarks.   72

CHAP. VI.

Names and descriptions of particular West India fruits which grow in the island; also of European and American fruits, herbs, vegetables, and flowers; with observations on their properties, &c.   86

CHAP.

CONTENTS.

CHAP. VII.

Of the trade of the island, previous to its reduction by the French last war, with a relation of that circumstance; and the articles of capitulation to which it surrendered. 104

CHAP. VIII.

Of the government of the island under the French, with a relation of the distressed situation of the English inhabitants, until its restoration to Great Britain; an account of that event, and several other subjects. 138

CHAP. IX.

An account of the division of the island into parishes and towns, with a description of its capital, the principal buildings, fortifications, and harbour; together with observations on Prince Rupert's Bay, and the grand Savannah in that island. 171

CHAP. X.

The civil government, officers, courts, and other subjects relative to them; also a description of the militia of that island. 195

CHAP. XI.

Description of the white inhabitants, free people of colour, and native Indians of the island; their manners and customs, with observations. 208

CHAP. XII.

Of the negro slaves of this island, their rebellion and reduction, the usage, manners, customs, and characters of these people in general in the West Indies. 224

CHAP. XIII.

Of the present trade of the island, and the free port of Roseau, with remarks. Conclusion. 276

THE

HISTORY

OF THE

ISLAND OF DOMINICA.

CHAPTER I.

DESCRIPTION OF THE ISLAND, ITS SITUATION, EXTENT, CLIMATE AND OTHER SUBJECTS; TOGETHER WITH AN ACCOUNT OF THE CONQUEST OF IT, ITS CESSION TO GREAT BRITAIN, AND THE DISPOSAL OF THE LANDS BY THE CROWN.

THE island of Dominica is situated in 15 degrees, 25 minutes, north latitude; 61 degrees, 15 minutes, west longitude from London; and 43 degrees, 40 minutes, from Ferro.

The discovery of this Island was claimed by the three kingdoms, of England, France, and Spain; but the right of possession remained undecided, and Dominica was considered as a neutral island, by three Crowns; till the year 1759, when, by conquest, it fell under the dominion of Great Britain; and was afterwards ceded to England, by the treaty of peace concluded at Paris, in February 1763.

On the cession of the island to the English, Commissioners were appointed under the Great Seal, and sent out there with authority, to sell and dispose of the lands by public sale, to English subjects, in allotments. "Of not " more than one hundred acres of such land " as was cleared; and not exceeding three " hundred acres in woods, to any one person, " who should be the best bidder for the same." These allotments were disposed of for the benefit of the Crown, and were confirmed to the purchaser, by grants, under the Great Seal of England;

THE

HISTORY

OF THE

ISLAND OF DOMINICA.

CHAPTER I.

DESCRIPTION OF THE ISLAND, ITS SITUATION, EXTENT, CLIMATE AND OTHER SUBJECTS; TOGETHER WITH AN ACCOUNT OF THE CONQUEST OF IT, ITS CESSION TO GREAT BRITAIN, AND THE DISPOSAL OF THE LANDS BY THE CROWN.

THE island of Dominica is situated in 15 degrees, 25 minutes, north latitude; 61 degrees, 15 minutes, west longitude from London; and 43 degrees, 40 minutes, from Ferro.

The discovery of this Island was claimed by the three kingdoms, of England, France, and Spain; but the right of possession remained undecided, and Dominica was considered as a neutral island, by three Crowns; till the year 1759, when, by conquest, it fell under the dominion of Great Britain; and was afterwards ceded to England, by the treaty of peace concluded at Paris, in February 1763.

On the cession of the island to the English, Commissioners were appointed under the Great Seal, and sent out there with authority, to sell and dispose of the lands by public sale, to English subjects, in allotments. "Of not "more than one hundred acres of such land "as was cleared; and not exceeding three "hundred acres in woods, to any one person, "who should be the best bidder for the same." These allotments were disposed of for the benefit of the Crown, and were confirmed to the purchaser, by grants, under the Great Seal of England;

England; with conditions in each grant, "That every purchaser should pay down "twenty per cent of the whole purchase mo- "ney, together with sixpence sterling per "acre, for the expence of surveying the land; "and that, the remainder of the purchase "money should be secured by bonds; to be "paid by equal installments, in the space of "five years, next after the date of the grant. "That, each purchaser should keep on the "lands so by him purchased, one white man, "or two white women for every hundred acres "of land, as it became cleared; for the pur- "pose of cultivating the same. Or in de- "fault thereof, or non payment of the re- "mainder of the purchase money, the lands "were to be forfeited to his Majesty, his "heirs and successors."

The Commissioners were also impowered to execute leases to the French inhabitants, of such lands as were found in their possession at the

the time of the surrender of the island; and which lands were thus leased to those inhabitants, who were desirous of keeping them in possession, on consideration of their taking the oaths of allegiance to his Britannic Majesty.

These leases were executed for a term, not less than seven, some fourteen, and others for forty years absolute; renewable at the time limitted for the expiration of the same. With conditions in every lease, " That the possessor, " his heirs or assigns, should pay to his Ma- " jesty, his heirs or successors, the sum of " two shillings sterling per annum, for every " acre of land, of which the lease should " consist." " And, that they should not sell " or dispose of their lands, without the con- " sent and approbation of the Governor, or " Commander in chief of that island, for the " time being."

The

The Commissioners were likewise impowered to make grants, under the Great Seal, of lots to poor settlers; to such English subjects, as should be deemed fit objects of his Majesty's bounty; in allotments of not more than thirty acres of land, to any one person. With authority also to the said Commissioners, to reserve and keep such lands, in the most convenient parts of the island as they should think proper for fortifications, and the use of his Majesty's army, and navy. Together with a boundary of fifty feet from the sea shore, round the whole island; and reserving all mines, of gold and silver, which might thereafter be discovered there, for the use of his Majesty, his heirs and successors [*].

This island is 29 miles in length, and 16 miles in breadth, but in some parts it

---

[*] It is the opinion of many people, that there are mines of both those metals in this island; particularly of silver; pieces of silver ore having been found in the interior N. E. part.

is broader, being of a very irregular figure. It is rugged and mountainous in some parts; but spacious plains, and fine extensive vallies are interspersed throughout the island, which are in general very productive.

The climate of this country is hot at times, in places on the sea coast, that are much sheltered by mountains; but in the open parts of the island, at no great distance from the sea shore, it is moderately cool at most times, and greatly resembles the climate of England, in summer. This is occasioned by the almost constant breezes blowing from the mountains, which moderating the heat, render it more supportable than it is, in those islands of the West Indies that are more level. In the interior mountainous parts, it is perfectly cool in general; owing to the vast quantity of tall woods, and the heavy rains which fall in those places, in some part or other almost every day; which render it so cold, in the night especially,

especially, that people who reside there are obliged to use woollen coverings on their beds, in the same quantity as in winter time in England *.

The climate is, however, reckoned very wholesome, especially in those places where invalids usually go for the recovery of their health, which is frequently re-established by a few weeks residence there. Besides, a good breeze generally blows from the mountains most part of the day, which greatly moderates the heat on the sea coast; and persons who live there temperately are seldom afflicted with the disorders, incident to most other West India islands.

* In the interior parts of this island, it is impossible to preserve salt in its proper state; for as soon as it is brought thither, it dissolves into a thick liquid, from the remarkable dampness of the air. This dampness is also prejudicial to articles of furniture that are glued, which frequently, after a long succession of rain, will fall to pieces.

The wet season in this country commonly sets in about the end of August, and continues till about the beginning of January, but with frequent intervals of fine weather. The severity of the rainy season, is usually in the months of September and October, when very heavy continual rain falls for days together; nay, it has been known to fall there for two or three weeks at a time, with very little intermission. The island, however, is seldom without rain, in some part or other; and often during a promising day, the disappointed traveller meets with such sudden, and heavy showers, that in an instant wet him to the skin, nor is an umbrella or great coat of much service, the rain falling in such large drops, and often accompanied with such severe gusts of wind, that the umbrella is rather an inconvenience; but let him be careful to change his wet cloaths as soon as possible, for inconsideration, in this respect, has proved fatal to many in this climate.

When the rains are violent and of long continuance, they do great mischief in the island, among the plantations; carrying away large tracts of land with coffee, plantain trees, sugar canes, and ground provisions; which are all hurried into the sea. In the towns also, they often do much damage, causing the rivers to overflow their banks, or breaking out in fresh places, carry away houses, or whatever else stands in the way of these dreadful torrents.

Thunder and lightening is seldom so severe in Dominica, or does so much damage there as in many other parts of the West Indies; although there have been some instances of lightening striking vessels in the road, damaging houses and killing people; but such instances are very rare.

Nor are earthquakes, those alarming phænomena of nature, so frequent, or so destructive in this, as in many other West India islands; yet,

yet, it is afferted by fome of the firft inhabitants, that earthquakes happened here formerly very frequently; efpecially foon after the Englifh firft took poffeffion of the country; when they were felt feverely, feveral times in a day, for the fpace of fome weeks together, which fo terrified the inhabitants, that they were on the point of quitting the place, but happily they foon fubfided. Thefe people fay likewife, that although no material damage happened at that time, yet that the ifland was fplit in feveral places; and in particular, a large chafm was made in a mountain there called Demoulins, fo very deep, that though they attempted with feveral coils of cordage fpliced together, yet they were unable to fathom it. There is, however, no appearance left of that remarkable circumftance, which yet by no means contradicts the veracity of their report.

Hurricanes, those dreadful scourges of the West Indies, are seldom very severe in Dominica; and in comparison with the mischief they generally do in other islands, may more properly be termed only heavy gusts of wind, especially when compared with the destruction done by that in the Leward islands the first of September, 1772; the most dreadful one that for some time has been felt in the West Indies. In the hurricane season, the damage received in Dominica is principally occasioned by the very heavy rains, or by the sea, which sometimes in those seasons tumbles into the bays, especially that of Roseau, in a very frightful manner; and making on the shore, overwhelms the vessels that unfortunately happen to be there at anchor; and sweeps away the houses, or whatever else is in the way of its destructive force.

A particular circumstance of this kind, which happened there the last day of September,

ber, 1780, was the most remarkable that has occurred in this island, in the memory of the oldest inhabitant, and did the most mischief. It did considerable damage among the plantations, and in Roseau destroyed several houses on the bay, and several vessels in the road.

The effects of these hurricanes in the West Indies are truly astonishing; for the wind, with a fury hardly credible, blowing from different points at one and the same instant, carries all before it; the rain is as it were taken out of the sea, and hurled on the land in clouds; which from not having time to exhale, is as salt as the briny element from which it was driven; and falls in drops as large as hail stones, affecting the hands and naked face, in the same manner as a severe hail storm; the whole of the scene is truly alarming and beyond description dreadful.

The

The mornings and evenings in Dominica are in general remarkably pleasant and cool; that is to say, from day break till eight o'clock in the morning, and between five and six o'clock till bed time in the evening. Early in the morning is the time, when those who can afford it, and wish to preserve their healths, will do well to employ their leisure time till breakfast, either riding on horseback, or taking a walk, to enjoy the cool, enlivening breezes. Bathing, previous to these exercises, is also the best preservative of health, and here people have the opportunity of doing it either in the rivers or in the sea.

Frequently bathing in cold water is productive of much benefit to persons in warm climates; as, exclusive of that which arises from cleanliness, so necessary in hot countries, it braces the nerves, and keeps the body refreshingly cool the whole day after. By taking a ride there on horseback, a person in the space of half an hour is tranfported from an uncomfortable warm air on the fea coaſt, to a pleaſantly cool retreat in the interior parts of the country; which, in an evening eſpecially, he may leiſurely enjoy, till diſpoſed to return to town; when the breezes, by that time ſet in to blow from the mountains, permit him to ſleep the remainder of the night in cool tranquillity.

The taking a morning or evening's walk in this iſland, by the ſides of the rivers, whoſe glaſſy ſurface glides ſwiftly on, or murmuring water-falls foam to the view, is very pleaſing. Does fancy lead him to enjoy the ſcene, a mile or two, he ſtill finds ample amuſement. Viewing the rapid ſtreams, he ſees the ſilvered fry, ſporting on its ſurface, in aſtoniſhing numbers. The ſerpentine windings of the rivers in ſome parts; in others, the waters wide, deep, and ſilently flowing along; and in many places, numberleſs falls of water, tumbling

bling down the sides of steep precipices, or rushing over the tops of huge stones in the beds of the rivers, at once charm both the sight and hearing. Is he fond of the delightful study of botany; here an extensive field is open for his speculation, and numberless curious shrubs, plants, and flowers, that grow spontaneously, afford him ample scope for enquiry?

Rising early in a morning in this country, you have the delightful pleasure of exploring the wonders of the heavens; the morning star, with a rapidity that exceeds all bounds of conception, running its daily course; the sun emerging from the sea, all glorious to behold; and in the words of the Psalmist, "Coming forth like a bridegroom out of his chamber;" and all the lesser planets twinkling into obscurity. In the evening in Dominica, is the most amazingly glorious scenery that can possibly be imagined; the heavens be-
spangled

spangled with innumerable ſtars, which the denſe climate of Europe hides from mortal ſight, or which are but barely to be diſtinguiſhed, are in this iſland open to full view; and the lovers of aſtronomy have there an opportunity to make new diſcoveries in that ſcience.

In the evenings, although the air is cool, yet it is not accompanied by thoſe noxious vapours, ſo remarkable for their dangerous effects in ſome parts of the Weſt Indies; ſo that it is not uncommon for people in this Iſland to ſit whole evenings in the open air, without any detriment to their healths.

CHAPTER II.

DESCRIPTION OF THE SOIL, MOUNTAINS, AND WOODS OF VALUABLE TIMBER, AND OTHER TREES: ALSO OF THE BIRDS OF THE WOODS, PECULIAR TO THE ISLAND.

THE Soil of Dominica, in some places, is a light, brown-coloured mould, that appears to have been washed down from the mountains, and mixed with decayed branches, and leaves of trees. In the level country, towards the sea coast, and in many places of the interior parts, it is a fine, deep, black mould, which is peculiarly adapted to the cultivation of the sugar cane, coffee, cocoa, and all other articles of West India produce. The under stratum of the soil is a yellow, or brick clay, in some parts, in others it is a stiff tarrace; but it is in most parts very stoney.

The land is in general very productive, especially in the interior parts, but towards the sea coast, it requires to be frequently manured; because the surface of it usually opens into large chasms in dry weather, thereby exposing the soil to the excessive heat of the sun; so that its vegetative quality can only be restored by dunging. This, however, is not very easily done by the greater part of the planters; because they have not in general a sufficient number of cattle on their plantations, in proportion to the land under cultivation, of the sugar cane in particular; from whence, in a great measure, and to the want of negroes, is to be attributed the small quantity of sugar exported from this settlement to England.

Several of the mountains of this island are continually burning with sulphur, of which they emit vast quantities. From these mountains issue numbers of springs of mineral

ral water, whose virtues are extolled for the cure of many disorders; in some places the water is so very hot, as to boil an egg, &c. in less time than boiling water, and this heat is retained at some distance from its source.

These sulphureous mountains are certainly among the most wonderful phænomena of nature, and command our astonishment and admiration. To see vast tracts of land on fire, whose smoke, like clouds, stretches far around; brimstone in flames, like streams of water issuing from the sides of precipices; in the vallies large holes full of bituminous matter, boiling and bubbling like a caldron; the earth trembling under the tread, and bursting out with loud explosions, are objects truly terrific to the beholders; who, on the spot, are struck with awe and admiration, on viewing such dreadful works of the Al-
mighty

mighty, who caufes them to exift, for purpofes only known by him *.

Others of the mountains are exceedingly large and high, whofe fummits, fides and feet are covered with vaft tall woods, which together with the under woods, are fo crouded as to be almoft impervious to the eye, and that for feveral miles around. From the tops and fides of thefe defcend numberlefs fprings and waterfalls, which form the moft delightfully romantic cafcades, of fine, cool, wholefome water, as clear as cryftal, excepting in places where it is tinctured with fulphur.

---

* In places where thefe fulphureous mountains are fituated, there is no poffibility of preferving articles of filver in their clean bright order, as they turn black and are not fit for ufe, unlefs cleared from a moifture that adheres to them. This is alfo perceptible to perfons having money in their pockets, buckles or buttons on their cloaths made of that metal; which will immediately on their coming thither turn black, from the powerfully quick effect of the fulphur on them.

The woods of Dominica, which constitute nearly two-thirds of the island at present, including the parts that are incapable of cultivation, on account of steep and rugged mountains, afford a vast fund of excellent timber: consisting of locus-wood, bullet-tree, mastic, cinnamon, rose-wood, yellow-sanders, bastard-mahogany, iron-wood, several species of cedar, and various other sorts of wood, useful for building houses, vessels and canoes, for furniture, for dying, and other necessary purposes.

In the woods, an awful, yet pleasing solitariness prevails; but that which makes them the more agreeably romantic, is the noise of falling waters, the whistling of the wind among the trees, the singing and chirping of an innumerable quantity of birds among the branches, and the uncommon cries of various kinds of harmless insects, which together with the dark shadiness of the trees, form a solemn but delightful scene for contemplation.

The trees in the woods are of uncommon height, and by far exceed in loftiness the tallest trees in England. In this island their tops seem to touch the clouds, which appear as if skimming swiftly over their upper branches; and looking up the trees is painful to the eye. Many of the trees are likewise of enormous girt, and their spreading boughs extend far around; those of the fig-tree especially, under whose inviting shade hundreds at a time may repose themselves, without fear of being wet by the heaviest shower of rain, or dread of the influence of the scorching sun-beams.

In the woods the trees are, in common, covered with different foliage, so that it is usual to see one tree dressed out with the rich liveries of several, all growing in beautiful variety:

variety: the trunk and branches, covered with ivy and other plants, growing on them like houſe-leeks.

That the leaves of different trees ſhould be found on one tree, is an object worthy of ſpeculation; but yet, in my opinion, is no other way to be accounted for, than by ſuppoſing that the ſeeds of different trees, being ſcattered by the wind, fall into the heart of the ſame plant, like houſe-leeks, and are thus incorporated into the tree on which they are ſeen growing.

The different ſpecies of ivy, or rather wild vines, in the woods, grow to a great ſize, and have the appearance of ſo many cords, or thick ropes, faſtened to the branches. Some of theſe are very tough, ſtrong, and uſeful; and hoops, baſkets, and other wicker utenſils are made of them: alſo walking-ſticks, called

ſupple-

supple-jacks, which, if cut in the proper season, are very durable, and so pliant, that both ends may be bent together without breaking them. These being in general regularly knotted, and of a good polish, are much admired for walking-sticks, or to use on horseback instead of whips; for both which purposes many of them are frequently sent to England, where they are well known.

Among other valuable trees in the woods of Dominica is the gum-tree, which yields great quantities of that article. The circumference of the body of this tree is generally very great, and its timber is, on that account, made into canoes; which is done by digging or burning out the inside, and shaping the log into form. The gum falls from the body and branches of the tree in great quantities, in substance like white wax, and was very serviceable to the planters of that island, during the time it was
in

in poſſeſſion of the French laſt war; this gum being uſed inſtead of oil, which could not then be had, to burn in lamps in the boiling houſes when making ſugar. The Romiſh prieſts of this iſland uſe it likewiſe in their cenſers at funerals, and other ceremonies of their church, it having a very aromatic ſmell when burning; and it is ſuppoſed to contain virtues which might be valuable in medicines, was it better known.

The timber alſo of this tree, as well as that of ſeveral others in the woods, makes good ſhingles for covering of houſes, and was very ſerviceable for making ſtaves for ſugar and coffee caſks, at the time the Americans refuſed ſupplying the Engliſh colonies with them. Several fine ſloops and ſchooners have likewiſe been built of the timber of this iſland; and the veſſels that have been built of it are eſteemed preferable

able, both for strength and durability, to others built of timber imported from North America.

Cabbage trees are in great plenty in Dominica, and are very serviceable on the plantations, as their trunks sawed, or split, make good laths or rails for cattle-pens, being very durable: the branches and leaves are used for thatching of houses; and the cabbage part of them is excellent eating. These trees are of great height, have much the appearance of the cocoa-nut tree, and bear a berry much like a date. The cabbage part is in the top, whence it is taken after the tree is cut down; and when that part is boiled it is equally as good, and tastes much like the bottom part of an artichoke. It also makes a very good pickle, some of which is often sent to England as presents.

The

The woods of Dominica abound with wild pigeons, mountain doves, ring-neck doves, ground doves, partridges, mackaws, parrots, hawks, diablotins, and a variety of finging and other fmall birds; among which is the mountain whiftler, the thrufh, and wren: from the finging, whiftling, and chirping of which, the woods refound in a moft delightful manner.

The wild pigeon is of the fize of the common houfe pigeon, has a red bill and legs, and its feathers are of a dark blue, tinged with a gold colour. They build on the tops of the higheft trees, lay only two eggs at a fitting, but hatch feveral times in the feafon, which is from February to Auguft. Their flefh is of a dark colour, and is very fat when they are in feafon, which is after their breeding time is over, when it has a moft delicious flavour, and is greatly relifhed.

The

The mountain dove is alfo nearly the fize of a houfe pigeon, has the fame red-coloured bill and legs, but its feathers are of a brown colour. It differs but little from the ring-neck dove, being only a fize larger, and builds its neft on trees in the mountains, or at the fides of fteep precipices, where it makes a pleafing, loud, plaintive noife. The ring-neck dove builds in coverts in the woods, as does alfo the partridge, which is likewife a fpecies of the dove kind, but from its great refemblance, it is called the pieddrié by the French. The flefh of the three kinds is much liked, but has a bitter tafte, as has that of moft other birds of the country, owing to the berries they feed on; this tafte, though at firft difagreeable, is foon relifhed by moft people, and they are reckoned very wholefome. The ground dove is not much bigger than a lark when ftripped of its feathers, which are of a brown colour. It has a red bill and legs, makes a pleafing plaintive noife, noise, and when killed in season its flesh is very fat, and of a delicious flavour; for which reason is is generally called the West-India ortolon.

The mackaw is of the parrot kind, but larger than the common parrot, and makes a more disagreeable, harsh noise. They are in great plenty, as are also parrots in this island; have both of them a delightful green and yellow plumage, with a scarlet-coloured fleshy substance from the ears to the root of the bill, of which colour is likewise the chief feathers of their wings and tails. They breed on the tops of the highest trees, where they feed on the berries in great numbers together; and are easily discovered by their loud chattering noise, which at a distance resembles human voices. The mackaws cannot be taught to articulate words; but the parrots of this country may, by taking pains with them when caught young. The flesh of both is eat, but being

very

very fat, it wastes in roasting, and eats dry and insipid; for which reason, they are chiefly used to make soup of, which is accounted very nutritive.

The hawks are of two kinds, the one of the largest size of those species, the other that of the small sort in England. They are both very ferocious, commit great depredations among the other birds in the woods, and on the plantations often destroy fowls and house pigeons.

The diablotin, so called by the French, from its uncommonly ugly appearance, is nearly the size of a duck, and is web-footed. It has a big round head, crooked bill like a hawk, and large full eyes like an owl. Its head, part of the neck, chief feathers of the wings and tail, are black; the other parts of its body are covered with a milk-white fine down; and its whole appearance

is

is perfectly singular. They feed on fish, flying in great flocks to the sea side in the night-time; and in their flight make a disagreeable loud noise like owls: which bird they also resemble, by their dislike of making their appearance in the day-time, when they are hid in holes in the mountains, where they are easily caught. This is done by stopping up some of the holes, which lead to their hiding places, and placing empty bags over the rest, which communicate under-ground with those stopped: the birds at their usual time of going forth to seek their food in the night-time, finding their passage impeded, make to the holes covered with the bags; into which entering, they are immediately caught; and great numbers of them taken in that manner in a short time. The flesh of the diablotin is much admired by the French, who used formerly to export great quantities of them salted, to Martinique and

other

other French islands; but the traffic was put a stop to by the Legislature of Dominica, who, by an Act made for apprehending runaway negroes, prohibited the taking of those birds: as before that time, the runaways being numerous in the woods, furnished great quantities of them, for which they had in return, from some ill-disposed white people, muskets, powder, and balls; which they made use of in murdering the English inhabitants on the plantations.

The mountain whistler is of the size of an English lark, and is remarkable only for its loud charming whistle, which resembles the human voice in the melodious notes; but which this bird varies in a most astonishing manner.

The thrush is nearly the size of that in England, and has much the same kind of whistle

whistle. The wren is also of the size and figure of those in England, and sings delightfully, especially early in the morning, and in the evening when other birds are at roost: for which reason it is by some, called the nightingale. What is remarkable of the singing birds of this country is, that they lose their singing faculties when taken, pine away and die, notwithstanding the greatest attention is paid to them.

There are also great numbers of owls in the woods of this island, and they make a most hideous, disagreeable noise in the nighttime. Swallows and bats are here likewise in great plenty; the latter breeding in hollow trees and in old houses; but it has not yet been discovered where the swallows breed, or retire to; yet they are frequently seen flying in great flocks during the wet season, and their appearance is reckoned a sure token of approaching rainy weather.

Dominica is visited in the hurricane months by wild ducks, curlews, plovers, and snipes; but not in such numbers at a time, as they are usually seen in some West India islands, owing to there being very few spots of stagnated water in this island, and to the great quantity of land in it still covered with woods.

Shortly after the reduction of this island by the French last war, the Marquis Duchilleau, then Governor, prohibited the killing of game during the breeding season. This prohibition has since been made into a law, by the English Legislature of Dominica, as a circumstance highly necessary; not only to prevent the runaway negroes from trafficking with that commodity for arms and ammunition, but also to preserve the game, which would probably have become extinct, if an unlimitted power of destroying them had not been restrained.

CHAPTER III.

OF THE RIVERS AND LAKES IN THE ISLAND, RIVER AND FRESH WATER FISH, ALSO OF SEA FISH, LAND CRABS, AND A DESCRIPTION OF THE NATIVE QUADRUPED, AND OTHER ANIMALS.

DOMINICA is well watered, there being upwards of thirty fine rivers in the island, besides great numbers of rivulets of excellent fresh water, but none of the rivers are navigable; yet, in the rainy season, they are sometimes very deep and rapid, coming down often in a frightful manner, carrying away considerable tracks of land, large trees, huge stones, and sometimes houses, into the sea.

The rivers and rivulets are plentifully stocked with excellent fish; the principal of which are, mullets, crocroes, pike, eels, suck-fish, and cray-fish, with which the tables of the inhabitants, especially those on the plantations, are well furnished; and much amusement is afforded to good anglers.

The mullet is of the shape of the sea-fish of the same name, and is often caught in the rivers of half a pound or more in weight; they are very fat and full of roe when in season, and are a great dainty.

The crocroe is an excellent fresh water fish, much of the shape of a trout, excepting the head, which in the crocroe is more round. Of these are caught, at times, some that will weigh from five to six, and usually from one to two pounds. The mullet and crocroe are generally caught with the hook and line, but sometimes they and other river fish are taken in the night-time by negroes, who, with a lighted torch made of a wood called " Bois chan-
" délle," which burns a long time, and which being held over the water, the fish, attracted

by

by the light, swim towards it on the surface, when they are chopped with cutlasses, and great quantities sometimes taken in that manner.

The pike is a rare fish, being found in one or two particular rivers only: they are sometimes caught of eight or ten pounds in weight, but they are not much esteemed, being reckoned unwholesome eating, as are also the different kinds of mud-fish, which are in great plenty in this island.

The eel is of the silver kind, and is an excellent fish, but are to be had in no great abundance. Of them are often caught some that will measure from two to three feet in length, and of a considerable thickness; when they are much esteemed, being very fat, and of a delicious flavour.

The suck-fish is small, but a very great dainty, and is remarkable for having a fleshy substance projecting from its navel, like the mouth of a purse, which has the faculty of suction, and by which the fish fastens itself so strongly to the stones in the rivers, that it is difficult to take them with the hook and line, to which they are often destructive: for this reason they are mostly caught with the hands groping among the stones; in which manner these fish are taken in great plenty by those who are dextrous at that way of fishing.

The cray-fish are of two kinds, the one approaching the size of the common lobster, the other that of the prawn. The first is much admired, but the latter having a rank, muddy taste, is not in much esteem.

But the chief dainty among the fresh-water fish in Dominica is the young frey, with which the rivers there are filled twice or thrice every year, and which are called by the French " Tréz tréz." These consist of various kinds of sea-fish just spawned, and with which that element swarms, for some miles distance from the shore, in numbers truly astonishing. These little creatures come into the rivers like a living stream, and in a short time swim two or three miles to an amazing height up the country. This they perform in a wonderful manner, skipping over such rapid streams, as repel their weak endeavours, from rock to rock, the surfaces of which are covered with them: or, seeking the smoothly gliding stream at the side of the banks, by degrees ascend the highest parts of the rivers.

The first day of the appearance of these frey in the rivers they are transparent and clear as crystal, so that every bone in them may be counted, and the movement of their vitals can be plainly discerned. The second day after, they lose much of that transparency; and the third or fourth day, it is wholly lost by by the nutriment which they feed on. They are caught in baskets, in which is put a tablecloth or sheet, and sinking the basket with stones, vast quantities are taken at a time. They are fried in a batter made of flour and milk, or stewed with herbs and spice. They are excellent food cooked either way.

Almost in the centre of the island, on the top of a very high mountain, surrounded by others above it, is a large natural pond, or rather lake of fresh water, which is also well stocked with fine fish, and it is said, is in some places unfathomable. It covers a space of some acres, spreads into three distinct branches, and has a very wonderful appearance in point of situation: it is about six miles distant from the town of Roseau, and great part of the road to it is a steep ascent. On first beholding this lake, a person becomes, as it were, rivetted for a time to the

the spot, with silent awe and admiration, at viewing so vast a body of water collected at such a height.

Dominica is likewise well supplied with excellent sea-fish; and the inhabitants have the advantage of procuring their fish almost as soon as caught, and often buy them alive in the market. Among the chief of the sea-fish are, groupers, cavallies, snappers, silks, baracutas, king-fish, Spanish mackrel, jacks, and sprats; the shell-fish are, lobsters, conks, wilks, and crabs; all which are so well known, as to render any description of them needless. Some few turtles are also caught at the windward part of the island; but this article is mostly brought hither from the Spanish islands.

This island is also remarkable for land-crabs, of which there are three sorts, white, black, and red. The first are distinguishable only for their poisonous quality,
which

which they acquire by feeding on the blossoms and leaves of the mahaut, a tree which gives name to a part of the island where it grows especially, and of which it is necessary to give first a description. This tree is of the cork kind, and grows spontaneously in watery places, or at the sides of rivers, and renders the water and air near them very unwholesome. They are about the size in common of the English oak-trees, and are almost continually in blossom; which is of a sickly yellow colour, and has much the appearance of the poppy blossom, but is rather larger. The body, branches, leaves, and blossoms of the mahaut-tree, contain a milky juice, which is a most subtle poison to every creature but the crabs who taste it; and to them it gives the same deadly quality if eaten, as has been fatally experienced by several persons. Yet notwithstanding their bad qualities, these trees are very serviceable, as the bark of them stripped off makes good ropes, nearly as strong as those

made

made of hemp; and the body and branches make floats for feins, or fishing-nets, equal to any made of cork, and as durable.

The black crabs are excellent, and safe eating, if caught in places where the Mahaut tree does not grow; particularly those brought from a part of the island, called "Souffrier;" where they are to be had nearly as large as sea crabs, and in great plenty. They are extremely fat when in season; and the females are full of a rich glutinous substance, called the eggs, which is perfectly delicious.

The red crabs are as small as the common sort of crabs in England, but are by far preferable to them; the females being full of the same rich glutinous substance as the black sort, when in season; at which time, the red crabs make their appearance in astonishing numbers: so that it is common for a person a person on horseback, to trample them under his horse's feet; and it is diverting to hear the rustling they make among the leaves on the ground, to get out of the way. Of these, and the black sort, is made a favourite dish, called there, pepper pot; which is made of crabs picked from the shells, stewed with Indian cale, and pods of Guinea pepper, and eat with a pudding made of Indian corn flour, or rice; this dish is esteemed by most of the inhabitants.

Some people have crab pens, or places made like fowl coops, for the purpose of keeping them alive, for some time after they are caught; feeding them with potatoe vines, Indian corn, herbage and water. This method is certainly the best to prevent the danger to be apprehended from eating them; as, notwithstanding the greatest caution in procuring them from particular places only, they have proved

fatal

fatal, by being imprudently eaten as foon as they were caught.

The land crabs are particularly deftructive to fugar plantations, when they are numerous, as they are on fome eftates near the fea; eating off the buds of the newly planted canes, of which they are very fond; as they are alfo of the Indian corn juft fprouted, of which they devour both blade and root. For this there is no remedy, but immediately replanting and catching as many of them as you can; for to attempt to ftop up their holes, which are numerous, as thofe of the mole; or to poifon them, would be vain.

There are no quadrupeds, natives of Dominica, except the Indian coney, which is nearly the fize of a rabbit when full grown. This animal is very fingular; its head, ears, eyes, nofe, mouth, and teeth, being exactly like thofe of a rat; and its body and legs like
thofe

those of a hog; the latter in particular, being hoofed like that animal. It has only a stump of a tail, which appears as if it was cut, but it is naturally so; and it is covered with long brown hair like hog's bristles, which it erects in the same manner when angry. It springs on its hind legs like a rabbit, and runs with great speed when pursued, making a noise like a Guinea pig.

These animals do much mischief among the ground provisions; which they root up in great abundance; feeding in herds, in the mornings and evenings, and are difficult to be shot, but are easily taken by dogs, or traps. Their flesh is not much admired for eating, it being dry, and in general rank; but to get rid of this taste, those who are fond of eating them, bury the dead animal in the ground for two or three hours previous to cooking it, which takes it off. They are sometimes kept alive as cu-
riosities,

riofities, and are foon tamed; but their urine is very offenfive.

There were formerly wild goats and hogs in the woods of this country; but they became fo by being let free on the plantations. There are, however, very few, if any, at prefent, having been moftly, if not entirely, deftroyed by the runaway negroes. The wild hogs were very dangerous when attacked, but their flefh delicious, owing to the vaft quantity and goodnefs of the wild yams, and other provifions, on which they lived, and which grow fpontaneoufly in the woods.

The feveral fpecies of four-footed animals which breed in Dominica are, horfes, horned cattle, fheep, hogs, goats, rabbits, and Guinea pigs. The poultry are, geefe, ducks, turkies, dunghill fowls, Guinea fowls, and houfe pigeons.

The

There are but few horses bred here; and they are no way remarkable, either for strength, beauty, or spirit; but are rather small and unsightly. This proceeds entirely from the want of good breeding mares and stallions, with proper persons competent in the knowledge of breeding and taking care of those useful animals; as the horses brought from England, America, and the other islands, thrive extremely well here.

The present pastures in this island are by no means extensive, although very good for cattle; consequently, there are but few of them. But those that are bred here are as strong, breed as well, and are as fine looking creatures, as in any part of the West-Indies.

Nor are sheep or goats in any great numbers in Dominica; but those of both species breed as well here as in any other island; and when
killed

killed for market, their flesh is tender, fat, and juicy, equalling in flavour that of venison. What is remarkable of the sheep in particular, is, that they retain their wool in this island much longer than in most other parts of the West Indies, where they shed their fleecy coats very soon after being brought to that climate, which causes them to change into fine long hair, as in goats.

Hogs are in tolerable plenty in the island, and may be raised in great abundance, the country being very favourable for breeding them, as it affords plenty of proper provisions: Their flesh is very white, firm, and fat, and of a delicious flavour, especially those raised on the plantations; but in the towns, where the hogs are suffered to go at large, and fed on any filth that falls in their way, their flesh is not so good.

Rabbits, Guinea pigs, and the different species of poultry, breed extremely well in Dominica, and are in as great perfection there as in any other part of the world.

CHAPTER IV.

OF THE MOST REMARKABLE REPTILES AND INSECTS OF THE ISLAND, THEIR VENOMOUS AND OTHER QUALITIES, WITH REMARKS.

THE principal and most remarkable of the reptiles and insects in Dominica are, snakes, lizards, wood-slaves, guanas, frogs, grugru worms, borer worms, centipedes, scorpions, spiders, sawyer flies, blacksmith flies, loggerhead flies, Spaniard flies, freemason flies, the wood-horse, and vegetable flies.

Some of the snakes are small, and others very large and thick. Of the last sort is that called by the French, "Tête du chien," or Dog's-head snake, from its head, which much resembles that of a dog. Some have been caught in this island that measured upwards of twelve feet in length, and as thick as a man's leg. They have long, sharp teeth; their skins are scaled and beautifully spotted, and they have at the end of their tails a blunt-pointed, horny substance, which enables them to climb the trees.

The bite of these snakes is not venomous, nor is that of any kind of them in this island; but the tête du chien does much mischief among the birds in the woods; and on the plantations they frequently devour the fowls and other poultry. They will swallow a full-grown fowl with its feathers; and several of them have been killed there with both a large fowl and an Indian coney entire in their bowels.

A remarkable circumstance, which happened in this island some time ago, deserves to be noticed in this place. A negro retiring from work one day at noon, instead of going home to get his dinner, fell asleep under a shady tree; and being missing at the time the other negroes assembled together to finish their daily

daily task, it caused a suspicion that some accident had befallen him; they accordingly went in search of him, and found him asleep, with one of his legs, up to the thick part of his thigh, in the jaws of a large snake. Awakened by their noise, he was in the greatest terror, and struggling to get disengaged, was severely bit by the animal; to prevent this as much as possible, wedges were placed between its jaws, whilst they cut it to pieces; by which means only he could be released. This operation took up some time, which together with the length of time, his leg and thigh had already been in the belly and jaws of the snake, reduced them almost to a state of digestion; and it was not till a considerable while after, that he recovered the intire use of them.

The fat of these snakes is esteemed an excellent remedy for the rheumatism, or for sprains, by rubbing it mixed with strong rum. Their flesh is eaten by many, particularly by the French, some of whom are very fond of it;

but it is reckoned unwholefome, and to occafion the leprofy.

The fkins of the tête du chien fnakes are excellent for covering fword-fheaths, or other inftrument cafes, for which purpofe they are in general ufed; but fome furgeons make ufe of them in medicine.

Lizards are very numerous in this ifland, and are of feveral kinds; fome of a green, others of a yellow, and fome beautifully fpotted with both colours. They are very harmlefs, feed on flies, worms, and other fmall infects, which render them very ferviceable on the plantations. The ground lizard, one of the largeft of that fpecies, and of a black colour, has lately been difcovered to be an excellent remedy for the leprofy, when made into broth.

The wood-flave is a fpecies of the lizard kind, but of a more hideous figure, and is reckoned to be venomous. Its head is fhaped like

like a dog's, its body is scaled and spotted like a toad's, it has four legs, which are claw-footed, and on each toe a sharp, crooked nail, like a bird's; it lashes with its tail, which drops from its body on the slightest touch; and its whole appearance is very disgusting.

They are commonly not more than three or four inches in length, but some are rather larger. Some say, that they fix their nails so fast in the flesh of those on whom they chance to fall, as not to be removed without cutting them out: others recommend throwing dry sand on the part, which disengages their nails, when they are easily shaken off. However, I never knew any injury happen from the wood-slave; I have had them drop on my cloaths from the cielings of rooms, where they are usually to be seen in the evening, in search of food. They are great enemies to spiders and cock-roaches, and they make a noise which somewhat resembles the cackling of a hen.

The guana is shaped like a crocodile, its head, body, feet, and tail, resembling those of that animal. It is of a green colour, but can change it at pleasure to a light ash colour, as it always does when alarmed. It has gills like a cock, but of a pale colour, and a horny substance, like the comb of that bird, reaching from its nose to the neck. It has strong sharp teeth, shaped like a lancet, with which it bites severely; its tail is also armed with strong, blunt points, with which it wounds the legs of those who take it, if they are not careful, as it lashes strongly with its tail, which is very supple, and nearly twice as long as the other part of its body.

This animal is commonly between two and three feet long, from the tip of the nose to the end of the tail; and when of that length, about four or five inches thick, especially the females, about the belly, when breeding; at which time they are full of eggs.

The flesh of the guana is excellent eating, and is cooked in the same manner as turtle, to which it is by many preferred; their eggs are also reckoned a great dainty. They are caught by a very curious method: by whistling, which lulls them asleep, when with a strong vine, or string, fastened at the end of a long stick in a slip knot, which is pulled gently over its head, and when a sudden jirk is given with the stick the animal is secured. They are very harmless, shy, and difficult to come near; and a person bit by them, or wounded with their tails, is under no apprehensions of danger from either.

The frogs, called by the French "Crapaux," are very numerous in Dominica, and are an article of food to both the French and English, many of whom prefer the crapaux to chickens. They make fricassees, and soup of them, and the latter is recommended to sick people, especially in consumptive cases.

The

The method of catching the crapaux is somewhat singular; it being done by means of lighted torches in the night-time, when they are out in search of food. This method is also used to catch the land-crabs, which, as well as the frogs, from some deficiency in their eye-sight, are unable to resist the light of a burning flame; or it so fascinates them, that they have not the power to stir from the spot; but stupified by its rays, they become an easy prey.

The grugru-worm is a species of the grub-worm, but is much larger than the common sort, and breeds in the trunks of decayed cabbage and cocoa-nut trees. These worms are eat by many people, who esteem them a great dainty, and eat them roasted, with a strong sauce made of lime-juice, salt, and Guinea pepper. They are like marrow, when cooked; but their head gives them an appearance not very inviting, the first time they are eaten; yet that disgust is soon overcome,

by

by their exceeding rich flavour, which those who are fond of them say, exceeds any yet tasted.

The borer-worm is also a species of the grub-worm, and is a most destructive reptile, especially to the sugar-cane, to which its ravages are principally confined. This worm is commonly about an inch in length, and of the thickness of a large caterpillar; it is produced from the egg of a kind of butterfly, or moth, and was first discovered in this island about ten years ago.

Its mouth has two strong, sharp teeth, in shape like a hog's tusks, with which it bites severely, and with such smartness, that putting the blade of a knife between them, it will champ the blade, so as to be distinctly heard, and will keep it so fast, as to make it difficult to take it away. With its teeth it penetrates the buds on the joints of the cane, working its way into the inside, where it devours

vours the whole substance, rendering the joint like a tube: after which, it works into another joint, which it consumes in like manner; and continuing its progress, at length destroys the whole cane.

The devastation which these worms make in a field of canes in a short time is astonishing; and although several methods have been tried to destroy them, yet none have been successful. If care was taken when the canes were young, on the first appearance of the borer among them, to rub their stems and leaves with a preparation of lime-water, or salt brine, mixed with soot and mashed pods of Guinea pepper, perhaps they might be destroyed; as by sprinkling some of this mixture on those worms it will instantly kill them.

Ants are great enemies to the borer when they can get at them, but they are much prevented by its excrement, which being like filings of wood, and of a gluey consistence, usually

usually fills up and secures their holes from the entrance of the ants. Yet having myself removed that impediment, by clearing away the dung, and putting a few ants to the hole, on going to the place some time after, I have seen them collected in great numbers, all busily employed carrying away in their mouths pieces of the borer, whom they had ferretted out of its hole and killed.

Centipedes, called by the English "Forty legs," and scorpions, are numerous in this island, especially in the woods, and in old houses. Of the former are often seen some that will measure eight or nine inches in length, and thick in proportion; but the generality of them do not exceed three inches long. They are very harmless, except when meddled with; neither then is their bite, or the sting of the scorpion of this country, so dangerous, as in many other West India islands.

They are caught and put into strong rum; and if the part bit or stung be rubbed with it, the pain is soon allayed, though the sting of the scorpion is at first exquisite, and hardly to be endured with temper.

Spiders are also here in great plenty, and of various kinds, some of them being much larger than any in England, their bodies are covered with a fine down like hair, and their mouths are armed with strong, sharp teeth, or forceps, with which they wound severely, but their bite is not venomous. Others are very small, and beautifully spotted with a variety of the most lively colours; and some have eyes in different parts of their bodies, but they are all harmless.

The sawyer fly, so called from its faculty of sawing asunder the branches of trees, whose substance is its food, is about three inches in length when full grown, and is a very singular insect. Its head has somewhat the appearance of that of an elephant, it having a horny bill, like the proboscis of that animal, bending upwards from the under part, with another, pointing downwards from the upper part of its head, both of a jet black, and of a fine polish. On the inner surface of the upper bill are raised points, like the teeth of a saw, which are used by the insect in the same manner. Its body is like that of a beetle, but considerably larger, with double wings, the inner of which is like coarse gauze; and its legs are armed at each joint with crooked, sharp nails, with the same on each toe, like a bird.

The process of this insect in sawing down branches of trees is really admirable, but it is hardly possible to form an idea of the manner of doing it without a description. This work it performs by encircling the branch with its bills, the points of which it fastens well into the wood, and turning round it briskly by the strength of its wings, which make a loud buzzing noise,

noiſe, it in a ſhort time ſaws the branch aſunder. They are by many called elephant flies, from the great reſemblance of their heads to that animal; they are perfectly harmleſs, and are caught only to be kept as curioſities.

The blackſmith fly, is ſo called from its making a noiſe reſembling in ſound the ſtriking on iron. In the centre of its back is a projecting horny point, and a crevice of the ſame nature on the hind part of the head, near the ſhoulders, which being ſtruck together by a jerk of the head and body, make a tinkling noiſe, that may be heard at a conſiderable diſtance; and ſo elaſtic is the membrane which joins the head and body together, that, if the inſect is laid on its back, it will ſpring to a tolerable height upwards, and fall directly on its legs. It differs very little from the beetle in ſhape or ſize, excepting in its elaſtic powers, and making ſo ſingular a noiſe.

The fire fly is a wonderful infect, for it has a luminous quality in its head (above the eyes) under each wing, and in its tail; which, when the infect is flying, has the appearance of so many lights of candles moving in the air: or, the lights of a coach or post-chaise in a dark night, travelling towards you at a brisk rate.

Some of these flies are as big as the top-joint of a man's thumb, others are much smaller; and the latter have that luminous quality only in their tails. They have a charming effect on the eye at night in the groves of the woods, where they are seen flying in all directions, like so many thousand sparkles of fire; forming one of the grandest spectacles of the kind that can be conceived, in Dominica's woods " that nightly shine with infect " lamps."

The larger sort are often caught for the novelty of the light they give; if two or three of them are put into a glafs, placed in a dark room, you may fee diftinctly any object there; or by holding a book clofe to the glafs in which they are, you may fee plainly to read the fmalleft print.

There is another quality remarkable in the fire flies, which is, that feveral of them being killed and mafhed together will produce the fame effect, and be as vifible in letters marked out on the walls of a dark room, as if done with artificial phofphorus; and this for a confiderable time after the flies are dead.

The loggerhead fly is a fpecies of the moth, from which it differs only in the uncommon largenefs of its head, and a fingular quality of tranfparency in its body; which latter is very remarkable, for placing this fly near to the light of a candle, you may plainly diftinguifh every part of its vitals, and diftinctly count every movement of them.

The

The Spaniard fly and free-mason fly are both of the wasp kind, but they differ from each other in size, shape, and also in the substance and curious manner of making their nests. The first is of the shape of a small bee, and builds its nest of a waxy matter, in the form of a small flat button full of holes, which it suspends by a silky ligament to the cielings of houses, or to the boughs of trees, where it has the benefit of the wind to vibrate to and fro.

The free-mason fly is exactly of the shape, size, and colour of a wasp, and builds its nest of mud, in the shape of organ barrels. It is curious to see these little creatures at work, they shew so much art and industry, some of them fetching the mud in their mouths, while others are forming their small cones, or filling them up when finished with numbers of various-coloured small spiders, which they also bring in their mouths, for food to their young when hatched.

That which is further remarkable of thefe flies is, that it appears they qualify the fpiders, by fome means, for remaining a long time in as perfect a ftate as the firft day they were immured in their cells; I have feen fpiders, fo immured for feveral weeks, as whole and perfect in fize, fhape, and colour, as when alive.

There is another fpecies of thefe flies, called galley wafps, which is double the fize and of a bright light-blue colour. Thefe have very long ftings, which are plainly to be feen when they are flying, with which they wound very feverely, caufing the blood to fpout out, as from the prick of a lancet.

The fting of thefe flies is very painful, and perfons have been thrown into fevers by being ftung feverely by them; but they are feldom offenfive, unlefs difturbed.

The wood-horfe, called by the negroes the fairy-horfe, is a very fingular infect. Its head is like that of a grafshopper, it has two horns, confiderably longer than its own body, which is about three inches, and of one continued thicknefs, like a large caterpillar. It has fix legs, which are raifed and doubled above its body, like the fpringing legs of a grafshopper, but they have not the fame power, ferving it only to walk with, which it does very faft. It has no wings, is of a deep green colour, and is perfectly harmlefs.

The vegetable fly is a remarkable infect. It is of the appearance and fize of a fmall cockchafer, and buries itfelf in the ground, where it dies, and from its body fprings up a fmall plant, which refembles a coffee-tree plant, only its leaves are much fmaller. The plant which fprings from this infect is often overlooked, from the fuppofition people have of its being no other than a coffee plant; but on examining it properly, the difference is eafily diftinguifhed, from the head, body, and

feet

feet of the infect appearing at the root, as perfect as when alive.

In the woods of Dominica are vast swarms of bees, which hive in the trees, and produce great quantities of wax and honey; both of which are equal in goodness to any of those articles to be had in Europe.

The musquitoes and sand flies are not so numerous, or so troublesome in this country, as they are in most parts of the West Indies, owing to there being but few spots of stagnated water, which breeds them.

The musquito is a species of the gnat kind, but rather smaller than the common gnat in England. The sand fly is not much larger than the head of a large pin, but is a very tormenting little insect in some islands, particularly to persons newly arrived from Europe.

Ants are very numerous in Dominica, and are of several sorts; as the large black ant, the brown ant, the red ant, the flying ant, and the wood ant. The latter is the most troublesome, as they are very destructive to trees, and the timber in houses; which they will reduce to dust in a short time, if suffered to take up their abode therein. The best method to prevent this is, to rub the timber with tar or turpentine, which hinders their attacking it, or, if already there, to sprinkle arsenic in their nests, which kills them.

The other sorts of ants are injurious only to particular articles, as new sown seed, the buds and fruit of trees, especially in dry seasons, when sometimes they cover the ground in such numbers, as is truly astonishing.

CHAPTER V.

AN ACCOUNT OF THE DIFFERENT ARTICLES OF WEST INDIA PRODUCE, RAISED IN THE ISLAND; THE NUMBER OF SUGAR AND COFFEE PLANTATIONS THEREIN, WITH REMARKS.

THE several articles of West India produce raised in Dominica for commerce are, sugar, rum, coffee, cocoa, and indigo.

There are not more than fifty sugar plantations at present in this island, above thirty estates of that description having been abandoned, owing to several causes; and among others, to the imprudence and mismanagement of some of the first proprietors of them; and to the great disadvantages this island laboured under, while it was in the possession of the French last war.

It was a great misfortune, that on the firſt ſettlement of this country by the Engliſh, ſo great a rage prevailed in the new ſettlers for having extenſive eſtates, as many of them were no ways qualified for the laborious taſk of eſtabliſhing a valuable property, by clearing the woods, and proceeding, not only to ſuperintend, but to get forward by degrees, with induſtry and œconomy.

They flattered themſelves, that without all this, in the courſe of a few years, their fortunes would be made, as they had very large eſtates; but they did not conſider the conſequences of borrowing money at eight per cent. which was allowed in Dominica at that time.—The forming new eſtates with new negroes, inſtead of ſeaſoned ones, at a time when that climate was, from the quantity of its wood, ſo unſettled, that it rained beſt part of the year.—The extra labour of making roads, and carrying materials for building, which took

took up at least eighteen months, before any produce could be planted.—Whilst in several instances, some of them spent the money, which was intended to forward their plantations, in unnecessary buildings; or in an unwarrantable luxury of living.

Others, from an unpardonable greediness, purchased, in the names of their acquaintances or families, several lots of land, each containing the number of acres limited in the grants; by which means, persons who would have been more fit settlers, were deprived of them; and large quantities of land thus purchased, are now in the same state (in woods) as they were, when first sold at the Commissioners sales nearly thirty years ago.

Another material cause, to which the reduction of sugar plantations in this island may be attributed, is, that several of the first English settlers, from a want of knowledge in
the

the choice of lands, proper for the immediate cultivation of the sugar-cane, had chosen such places in the interior parts of the country, as were on the tops of high mountains, or surrounded by vast woods; which affording too much shelter from the sun, and being subject to too frequent great rains, chilled the canes, rendering their juice unfit for making sugar. Not but that, was the whole of the cultivable lands there to be cleared of their woods, there are few situations, even in the most interior parts, but would be proper for the growth of that article.

By this imprudent conduct of such of the new settlers, after they had spent considerable sums of money, which they had borrowed on the credit of their plantations so situated, and having lost a number of negroes and cattle by the dampness of the climate in those places, together with the difficult and laborious roads to them, they were at length driven to the necessity

cessity of abandoning their possessions to the mortgagees in Europe.

These latter, it is presumed, having taken an unfavourable opinion of the mortgaged premises, from having been sufferers already in the loss of considerable sums they had lent on them; and not knowing, or not considering the value of such property at a future period, are unwilling to advance more; at least the majority of the mortgagees seem to be disposed to let their lands remain in the same neglected, abandoned situation they have been in these several years past, to the great hindrance of the prosperity of that valuable island, as well as their own detriment.

It is computed, that on an average, one year with another, there are not more than three thousand hogsheads of sugar made annually in Dominica. This is certainly a very small

small quantity of that article for such an extensive island, or even for the number of plantations in it, at present under cultivation: for, supposing these fifty estates contained only two thousand acres of land in canes, which is a very small calculation, as several single estates have upwards of one hundred acres, and few less than sixty: this is at the rate only of a hogshead and a half per acre.

In the English old settled islands, three hogsheads of sugar for every acre in canes, on an average, is considered as a very moderate produce; for, after good seasonable weather previous to the crop, some lands have been known to yield from four to five hogsheads per acre. From the great disproportion in point of yielding, between the lands of other islands and those of Dominica, the superior fertility of the former may be inferred; which, however, is by no means the case: for the lands of the old islands, from having been a considerable number of years under cultivation, are so much worn out, as to require great attention to make them bear the culture of the sugar-cane. And the Planters there are obliged to let the land lie a year or two fallow occasionally, or only plant such vegetables as yams and potatoes, the roots of which open and enrich the soil; beside, it must be well dunged previous to planting.

Again, no more than one-half in some plantations, in others only one-third part of the land is yearly planted with canes; the other part being prepared for growing rattoons, turned into pasture for cattle, or given to the negroes for gardens, in order to improve and render it fit for the canes. The rattoons, it is necessary to acquaint the readers, who may probably not know the sugar-cane, are second canes, which spring from the roots of plant canes, after they have been cut down and

made

made fugar of; which the rattoons produce in like manner, but generally not in an equal quantity with the other. Of thefe, the lands of the old iflands will bear but one crop, in Dominica they will rattoon four or five years running, and the laft year's yielding of fugar will be as great as the firft.

The fugar eftates in the old iflands have generally a number of barren fpots in them, called " Yellow fpots ;" the fterility of which no art can overcome fo as to make them bear canes to any perfection ; for though they will fpring up, yet they foon change from a green to a yellow colour, and rot in the ground. And, moreover, the old iflands are frequently fubject to long and fevere droughts, which never happen in Dominica; and there is every reafon to fuppofe they never will, from the great number and heighth of its mountains, together with the vaft quantity of woods, which it will be next to impoffible

ever

ever to clear away in some parts of the island.

The land of Dominica is quite new, very little of it having been more than thirty years under cultivation, and a great part of it, it is probable, never since the creation; the soil thereof produces vegetation so quick, that it is truly amazing; and this vigour is particularly conspicuous in the sugar-cane, for it has been seen there of the length of sixteen feet and upwards, and double the thickness that it in general attain in other islands.

The lands on the sea-coast have abundantly the advantage of the interior country, for forming sugar estates; but then, they are contiguous to, or are overtopped by vast woods, and have not the benefit of an uninterrupted, warm air, which is necessary for the growth of canes to any perfection. Besides, the damps from the woods near them, rising in heavy fogs,

fogs, has a bad effect on canes; and though the lands on the sea-coast all lie on a declivity, yet the under stratum of the soil being either a stiff clay, or strong terrace, so much water is retained from the frequent rains, occasioned by the woods, as to chill the soil.

These considerations seem to point out the necessity, in order to render Dominica a good sugar country, of clearing the extensive forests of trees in the interior parts of it. When this is done, and not till then, will this island be distinguished for the number of its sugar plantations, and for the quantity of sugar it is absolutely capable of raising.

There are above two hundred coffee plantations in Dominica; but the principal and most productive of them belong to French proprietors, who raise great quantities of coffee, which they dispose of to the English merchants, who export it to Europe. There are, however, several valuable estates of that description belonging to the English inhabitants of it; and the coffee produced in this island is esteemed superior to that of most others in the West Indies.

It is computed, that, one year with another, there are between four and five millions of pounds weight of that article produced, and exported annually from this island to Great Britain, where it sells from 4l. 15s. to 5l. 5s. per hundred weight.

The cultivation of cocoa is not much attended to by the English planters; and the small quantity which is exported, is chiefly raised on the plantations of the French inhabitants.

Indigo is manufactured on only two or three English estates in the island; but they have lately very much neglected that article, owing to to too frequent rains, occasioned by the extensive woods.

Cotton trees thrive extremely well in the land on the sea-coasts of Dominica, but the cultivation of them is, at present, wholly neglected; as is also that of ginger. The latter having been formerly planted in estates that are now abandoned, it grows there spontaneously, and in great luxuriance.

The cassia-fistula, and castor-oil nut trees, are both raised on some plantations, but very little of the produce of either is exported. The cassia-fistula was considered by the French as so valuable an article, that soon after they were in possession of Dominica last war, an ordinance of the French King was proclaimed in Roseau, for every planter in the country to give in an account of the number of cassia-fistula trees he had growing on his estate.

Tobacco grows in great perfection, but it is only cultivated by the negroes, who raise it in their gardens for their own use.

Dominica is, beyond dispute, the most valuable island belonging to Great Britain in that part of the world, for the vast quantities and excellency of the farinaceous fruits and roots of the West Indies; such as plantains, bananas, manioc, or cassada, yams, sweet potatoes, cushcushes, tanias, eddoes, &c. &c. some of which are not to be found in the other islands, but which grow spontaneously in the woods of this. Among these are, the wild yams, which grow there in great abundance, and were the chief food of the runaway negroes for a number of years, till it became necessary to reduce them.

Also Guinea corn, Indian corn, and rice, grow extremely well in Dominica; the latter especially, which being introduced there by the American refugees, flourishes in the moist, flat lands, and yields in great perfection. The large plantations there of plantains and bananas, exceed any thing of the kind in the old islands; the inhabitants of which are often obliged to have recourse to this country for a supply of those fruits.

CHAPTER VI.

NAMES AND DESCRIPTIONS OF PARTICULAR WEST INDIA FRUITS WHICH GROW IN THE ISLAND; ALSO OF EUROPEAN AND AMERICAN FRUITS, HERBS, VEGETABLES, AND FLOWERS; WITH OBSERVATIONS ON THEIR PROPERTIES, &c.

THE island of Dominica produces every species of fruit peculiar to the West Indies; all which grow there in great perfection. The principal are, oranges, lemons, limes, citrons, shaddocks, water lemons, granadillas, sappadillas, pomegranates, alligator pears, mountain pears, pine apples, rose apples, star apples, sugar apples, custard apples, mamma apples, guavas, sea-side grapes, cocoa nuts, conk nuts, sourfops, papaws, cashew apples, and tamerinds.

The oranges in this island are of three sorts, the China orange, the bergamot, and the
Seville

Seville orange. The first sort is far superior, in flavour and sweetness, to any fruit of the kind to be had in England; the bergamot orange is small, but it is a most delicious fruit; and the Seville orange is very serviceable. The blossoms of their trees have a delighting fragrant smell, which is to be scented at a great distance; and the fruit, when ripe and full on them, has a very pleasing appearance.

The lemon and lime trees bear also very aromatic, scenting blossoms; and the fruit of both is in great abundance, large, and of an excellent quality. Of these, the latter especially, great quantities are often sent in barrels to England and America; the neighbouring English islands are likewise often supplied with them from this country, especially those of Antigua and Barbadoes.

The citrons are large, but are chiefly valuable for their rinds, as with them are made the best kind of sweetmeats.

The shaddocks are of two sorts, the one white in the inside, the other red; they are a large fruit, some of them being as big as a good sized musk-melon; but the red sort of them is most admired. The juice is contained in separate divisions of a thin, skin-like substance, as transparent as diamonds, and which have much the look of them, finely squared and polished. It has a sweet taste, tinctured with a bitter, and when the fruit is ripe is very agreeable, and reckoned a good addition to a glass of Madeira wine after dinner. The rinds of them also make good sweetmeats.

The water lemon is a fine fruit, of the shape and size of a dunghill fowl's egg. The rind of it is of a bright yellow colour, the

inside

inside is full of small, flat seeds, covered with a juicy pulp, which has a very agreeable, musky taste. It grows on a vine, which bears a very beautiful blossom, very much resembling the passion flower; and the vine is much admired, because it affords the most delightful shade when turned over an arbour.

The granadilla is rather larger than the the largest sized Lisbon lemon, and is an excellent fruit. It also grows on a vine, which bears a delightful sky-blue and yellow blossom, very fragrant, and of the same appearance as that of the water lemon, but much larger. The rind of the fruit is also of a yellow colour, but not so bright as the other; and the inside is full of seeds covered with a juicy pulp, but not of so musky a taste. The granadilla is much recommended to people in fevers, its juice being very cooling. The rind of it mixed with a little lime-juice, makes an excellent tart, nearly equal to those made with

English

English apples; and so very refreshing is the scent of these fruits, that many people suffer them to decay on their side-boards, for the sake of their agreeable smell.

The sappadilla is of the size and make of a bergamot pear, its juice is of a gluey nature, and of a sweet taste. The tree which bears it resembles a pear-tree, and its timber is very serviceable for mills, or to make cart-wheels of.

The pomegranates in Dominica are not so large as those brought to England from other countries; but they are fleshy, sweet, and good, when thoroughly ripe. They bear a delightful scarlet-coloured blossom, which, in size and make, is very like the flowers called blue-bottles; and the skin, or shell of the fruit, being boiled into a decoction, is given to persons afflicted with the flux.

The

The alligator pear is of the shape of an English bell pear, but is much larger. There are two sorts of this fruit, the one of a purple-coloured rind, the other of a pale green: the latter is the largest, and most esteemed. They are excellent fruit, and are greedily eaten by all kinds of animals; for even horses, who are in general not fond of fruit, will eagerly eat them. This is the fruit which is called in the West Indies "Vegetable marrow," from its rich melting taste, and it is justly reckoned the best and most wholesome fruit of the country.

Some people eat them with salt and black pepper, others with lime-juice and syrup, and some without either; but the generality of the French eat them with fish or flesh, with which they are very relishing. The seed of the alligator pear, which is nearly one-third part of the fruit, and shakes within it when ripe, has the appearance of the inside part of a horse-chesnut, chefnut, and has a very firm colour; for which reafon it is commonly ufed to mark linen with. This is done, by covering the feed with the cloth, and pricking out the letters with a pin; the juice filling up the punctures, ftains the form of the letters fo durably, that they are not to be wafhed out, only decaying with the cloth.

The mountain pear is found growing only on barren heights, or on the fides of fteep precipices; it grows on a tall, fluted-like ftalk, that has the appearance of a well-wrought, fluted, flender pillar, full of ftrong, fharp prickles. The fruit is of the fize of a pippin, its fkin is of a beautiful crimfon colour; when this pear is cut open, it prefents an innumerable quantity of fine black feeds, which are covered with a juicy pulp of the fame colour as the fkin, its tafte is much like that of a ftrawberry; by which name the fruit is fometimes called.

Pine apples grow in Dominica to a great size, and are in general very juicy, but they are not so good as in most other islands, owing to the too great moisture of the ground, which makes them grow too luxuriant and watry. Pine apples sliced, covered with brown sugar, and left some time to drain out their juice, make an excellent drink, after being strained, and set by for a time in bottles.

The rose apple is chiefly esteemed for its fine scent, which resembles that of the flower after which it is called. It is, however, eat by many, but is reckoned unwholesome; being put up with linen, it gives it an agreeable scent, equal to that of lavender.

The star apple, so called from the blossoms of the tree which bears it, resembling a star, is a fine fruit, of the size and shape of a large plumb, of a purple colour; and its juice is of an agreeably sweet taste, and of a gluey nature.

The sugar apple is a singular fruit, about the size of a middling-sized English apple, but in appearance differs from any fruit of that name, as it does also in quality. The rind of it is crossed in divisions, the shape of diamonds in a card, which are considerably raised above the furrows between each, and stand in regular rows. The outside is of a pale green colour, the inside has a great number of hard, black seeds, which are nearly as big as peas, and are covered with a moist, gritty pulp, which has the taste of sugar; and it is reckoned very wholesome.

The custard apple is of much the same nature with the former, only the skin of it is smooth, of a rust colour, and the inside pulp less gritty, resembling in taste a custard, after which it is called.

The mamma apple is a large fruit, of the size in general of a middling-sized musk melon, but some are much smaller. The rind of it is thick, strong, and has the appearance of leather; the inside has three large nuts, or kernels, which are covered with a thick substance, of the colour of a carrot, very juicy, and in taste much resembling that of a peach. It is a delicious fruit when ripe, but is reckoned to be unwholesome, from its indigestive quality, yet they make tarts of it. The timber of the tree which bears the mamma apple is a very beautiful wood, durable, and is used for furniture.

Guavas are of three sorts, the white, the red, and the yellow guava; the first is the largest and most esteemed, but they are all very good. The white sort grows in general as large as a good-sized apple, the red rather smaller, and the yellow about the size of a golden pippin, which they also much resemble.
The

The outside of these fruits is much like that of an apple, especially when half ripe, when they are used to make puddings or tarts of, which they make equal to an English apple, and are by many preferred. The inside of them is full of small, hard, and indigestible seeds, that are taken out when prepared for pastry, or for jelly; which latter they make in great perfection, and exceeding any thing of the kind.

The guava tree is of the shrub kind, but some of them grow tolerably large and lofty, especially those which bear the white guavas. Their timber and branches are very serviceable; and being durable, and of a supple nature, are used for making bows for cattle yokes, knees for canoes, or boats, baskets, &c. These trees have a singular property in them, as they are to be seen bearing ripe fruit, fruit just left by the blossoms, and blossoms in full bloom, all growing on the same branch.

The

The blossoms close during the night, but being touched with the hand, or receiving the heat of the sun in the morning, they expand, diffusing the most delightful, fragrant scent.

The sea-side grapes are of the size of other grapes, but are the produce of a large spreading tree, which bears them in small clusters. They have only one seed, which is nearly as large as the fruit, by which it is covered very thinly; have a very agreeable taste, but are of an astringent nature.

The cocoa nut is so well known, as to need no description; but they are not in such great plenty in Dominica, as in many other islands, owing to the little pains taken to plant them.

The conk nut is rather larger than a walnut, but grows from a vine, the blossoms of which are much like those of the water lemon. It has a thick, strong shell, full of seeds, like the water lemon, but the juice of it is not so sweet.

The soursop is a fine fruit, large, and much of the shape of an heart. When unripe, it is of a brown colour, and its skin is covered with raised points like prickles, but they are not sharp. When ripe, it is of a fine green colour, the points fall off, and the skin is quite smooth. It is a very wholesome fruit, in taste resembling fine cotton dipped in syrup, with a little tincture of acid, of a very agreeable musky flavour, and much recommended in fevers.

The fruit and the leaves of the soursop have a very singular quality in them, for the fruit will rot on the ground without the least visible appearance of worms, although most animals and birds are very fond of it; and the leaves being scattered in a room infested with fleas, soon clears it of those troublesome guests, by the

the strength of the smell of the leaves, which, however, is very pleasant.

The papaw apples grow in clusters on stalks, but each of them, when full-grown, is larger than the largest-sized English apple, some nearly as large as a good-sized musk melon, and have nearly the same look. When half-ripe, they are used as a vegetable, and boiled, are a good substitute for turnips; when full-ripe, they are a great antidote to worms, and are recommended to persons afflicted with them: the seeds of the apple especially, which have a hot quality, like pepper, are reckoned good in that disorder.

The blossoms of the papaw tree are of a beautiful white and yellow colour, have a very odoriferous scent, and with the stalks are made pickles and preserves of. The juice of the apples, which, when they are unripe, is like thick milk, has the peculiar quality of

making

making tough meat tender, by being rubbed over with it.

The cashew apples grow of different forms, sizes, and colours, some being shaped like a quince, and of the same colour, some longer, more round, less, and of a purple colour, and others of both colours; but all have the same astringent quality as the quince. These apples have each a nut, which grows out in the middle of their tops, and is of the shape of a kidney; the shell of which nut contains an oil of a corrosive quality that will consume iron; and being rubbed on the skin of a person, it will cause it to blister, as if burnt or scalded. The apple is usually roasted, the juice pressed out, and put hot into punch, to which it gives a very fine flavour. The nut is also roasted, and the kernel of it is esteemed preferable to that of any other nut whatever. Of these nuts, quantities are often sent from this island to England as presents.

The

The tamarind trees grow here in great perfection, and the fruit of them is excellent, being much used in medicine, for which purpose they are very valuable, and the timber of the trees is very serviceable.

English and American apple trees grow well in Dominica, and several of them are on different plantations in the island; particularly on those of Alexander Stewart, Esq. William Urban Bueé, merchant, and on some French estates, where the trees bear a juicy, well-flavoured apple.

Also strawberries, rasberries, and several other European and American fruits grow here in great perfection; proving, beyond a doubt, that was a proper attention to be paid to the further settlement of this island, there is hardly any description of foreign fruits but what would flourish in this country.

The gardens produce the black and green muscadine grapes, figs, musk melons, water melons, cucumbers, gourds, pompions, English, American, and West India beans and peas, cabbages, carrots, turnips, parsnips, lettuces, radishes, horse-radish, asparagus, artichokes, spinage, celery, onions, eschallots, thyme, sage, mint, rue, balm, parsley, and all sorts of vegetables and herbs, all which grow in this island in great perfection.

The flowers are, roses, tuberoses, pinks, jessamines, and several other sorts peculiar to the island; which latter grow spontaneously; some are very curious, and most of them have a very odoriferous smell.

The sensitive plant grows there spontaneously, and in great abundance; also the ipecacuanha, and the latter is often fatal to horses, cattle, and sheep, who chance to bite of it in feeding;

ing; for which reason it is necessary to eradicate it as much as possible out of the pastures. This plant bears very beautiful, scarlet and yellow flowers, which, with the leaves, are put into boiling water, and given as an emetic; but, without great experience, this method of using them is dangerous, and has proved fatal to many, who imprudently took too great a quantity of the infusion; for which reason great care should be taken in using it.

CHAPTER VII.

CONTAINS AN ACCOUNT OF THE TRADE OF THE ISLAND, PREVIOUS TO THE REDUCTION THEREOF BY THE FRENCH LAST WAR, WITH A RELATION OF THAT CIRCUMSTANCE; TOGETHER WITH THE ARTICLES OF CAPITULATION BY WHICH IT SURRENDERED.

DURING the space of the last five years, prior to the breaking out of the disturbances in North America, the island of Dominica was in a very flourishing situation. The port of Roseau, which was then a free port, was resorted to by traders from most of the foreign West India islands, as well as from England and North America.

The French and Spaniards purchased in this island great numbers of negroes for the supply of their settlements, together with great quantities of merchandize of the manufactures of Great Britain. These they paid for in gold and silver, or gave in exchange Muscovada and clayed sugar, coffee, cotton, gums, spices, ivory, mahogany, and dying-woods, the produce of their islands; all of which articles were exported to Great Britain in English bottoms; and thereby were productive of great advantages to the trade and navigation of the mother country.

The Americans imported thither lumber, boards, shingles, wood-hoops, staves, tobacco, flour, rice, salt-fish, horses, cattle, sheep, hogs, and feathered stock, the produce of North America. These were necessary articles for the new settlers, who paid for them in rum and molasses; or such other produce of the island as was at that time permitted to be exported in American vessels from the British West Indies.

The

The merchants of Dominica were then numerous, and were enabled to make regular yearly remittances, of confiderable value, to their correfpondents in England; and the planters of the country were furnifhed with the means of carrying on the fettlement of their plantations with vigour.

Soon after the commencement of hoftilities in America, and directly on the adoption of meafures by the Americans by way of reprifal, the trade of Dominica to and with America was finally ended, and drew with it the lofs of that, with the foreign Weft India iflands.

This total ruin of trade was attended with ferious confequences, fatal to the welfare of this ifland in particular, as being then only in a ftate of infancy with refpect to its fettlement; and it has never fince been able to recover its former flourifhing fituation: for the merchants, tradefmen, and others, having no

fale

sale for their commodities, or work in their line of business, withdrew themselves to places where trade and commerce were more brisk; and the planters, from being deprived of the means of furnishing themselves with such articles as were immediately necessary for their new estates, were driven to abandon, or to postpone the further improvement of them.

In this deplorable state was the island of Dominica when it fell into the hands of the French on the 7th day of September, 1778. Some months previous to this calamitous event his Excellency, Thomas Shirley, Esq. then Commander in chief of the island, knowing the defenceless state it was in, and being apprehensive it would be attacked, in case of a rupture with France, which was then threatened, employed a number of men for the defence of fort Cashacrou; distributed the few soldiers then in garrison into such places as

were

were thought neceſſary, and took every precaution in his power to prevent a ſudden attack.

Fort Caſhacrou, at that time the chief place of defence in the iſland, is ſituated on a rock of about three hundred feet perpendicular, and is ſurrounded on three ſides by the ſea, being joined to the main land by only a narrow neck of land, which renders it ſo very defenſible, that if well provided, a few men might keep it againſt as many thouſands.

This meaſure, therefore, of Governor Shirley, who guarded this fort, reflects great credit upon him; and the conſequences which happened ſoon after he quitted that government, from not purſuing his plan, is a laſting proof of his abilities.

About three weeks before the attack, a report prevailing that hoſtilities between England and France were actually commenced in Europe,

Europe, some attempts were made to put the island into a posture of defence. The soldiers, of whom there were only ninety-four, inclusive of officers, were stationed at the forts in and above Roseau, and a few of them at Cashacrou; the militia mounted guard in that town, and patrolled the streets every night till daylight, and every step, that seemed necessary, was taken to prevent a surprize.

Saturday, the fifth day of September, that year, was the day of meeting for the militia to perform their exercise in the field; and it was remarked, that they went through their evolutions with a degree of celerity, nearly equal to regular troops.

Among the spectators in the field, on this occasion, were several French strangers from the island of Martinique, and among them was an officer of that nation of the name of Gabrouse, who was afterwards harbour-master of of the port of Roseau. These strangers were in quality of visitants to some of their acquaintances in the island; but their business was, in fact, to see what state the place was in, and to engage the non-resistance of the French inhabitants against the then meditated attack, as it appeared afterwards by the public boast of the said Gabrouse. However, in consequence of some intimation to the Lieutenant-governor, that officer was taken up as a spy; but after a slight examination he was suffered to depart; and the report of his being in that capacity was treated with unmerited contempt.

It is worth while remarking in this place, that there seems to have been a degree of fatality attending this island at that particular period, as, exclusive of the men placed by Governor Shirley at fort Cashacrou, being discharged from that service soon after his departure for England, some months before the invasion,

vasion, every method was taken that could be thought of to guard against that event: and it was the determination of the English inhabitants, that should the island fall into the hands of the enemy, it should not be owing to their want of attention, or endeavours to prevent it.

But it so happened, and probably for wise purposes of Providence, as there is hardly a doubt but that the lives of many by that means were preserved, which would otherwise have been lost in the defence they certainly would have made, had they had timely notice to prepare for opposing the invading enemy.

This neglect of theirs was never so very conspicuous as on the last two days before the attack; for on the preceding Saturday, most of them were that evening at a public comedy acted in Roseau; and on Sunday evening, when the militia guard were composed of the chief civil officers and principal inhabitants, who turned out volunteers in that service; being unused to the hardships attending patrolling the streets all night, and watching to give notice of approaching danger, they preferred the more inviting enjoyments of diversions and good cheer in the guard-room; where, overcome by these amusements, between two and three o'clock in the morning they all retired to their own homes, wholly unapprehensive of further danger for that time.

This same evening, some ill-disposed French inhabitants found means to insinuate themselves into Cashacrou fort, where they contrived to make the few soldiers there on duty intoxicated with liquor, and afterwards filled up the touch-holes of the cannon with sand; so that when it was stormed by the French the next morning it was easily taken, and two of the English soldiers paid

paid dearly, the confequence of their great imprudence, by the lofs of their lives; being driven, with fixed bayonets, over the ramparts of the fort, and dafhed to pieces by the rocks at the foot of it.

The enemy began the attack between three and four o'clock in the morning of Monday, the feventh of September that year; but they had intended to have made their invafion much earlier, having fet out on the expedition from Martinique between the fame hours the preceding evening, but were detained by calm weather in the channel between the two iflands.

This was a very providential event for the Englifh inhabitants of Dominica, as there is every reafon to believe, that had the attack been made an hour fooner than it was, many of them would have been maffacred in their beds; if not by the French foldiers, there was every probability to apprehend it would have been done by a lawless banditti, composed of renegado white men, negros, mulattos, and the outcasts of society from several French and other foreign islands; who, with large knives and pistols stuck in their belts, were prepared for the perpetration of every species of rapine, barbarity, and murder. These wretches, upwards of one thousand in number, were obliged to be satisfied for their failure of plunder on this occasion, by a contribution laid on the inhabitants by the Marquis de Bouillé, of four thousand four hundred pounds current money, which was distributed among them a few days after the surrender of the island.

After the enemy were in possession of Cashacrou fort, in the manner before noticed, the major part of their forces being still at sea, those that were landed either judging it imprudent to advance to Roseau, or being satisfied with

with their then succefs, they fired off two guns from that fort, and let off several skyrockets, as signals to their friends. This was likewise the first notice the inhabitants had of the attack, which was immediately announced, by firing an alarm gun, and beating to arms in the town.

Then was to be seen, visibly, the most poignant distress: the helpless women and children running, shrieking and crying through the streets; some of the women with their infants in their arms, others with such things of value as they could carry; the negroes terrified, running here and there,—all was, for a time, confusion, hurry, dread, and dismay, none knowing where to fly for safety from the invading enemy.

The situation of the white women and their children was, at that time particularly, pitiable; for, deprived of the protection of their husbands and fathers, who were obliged to leave them to go into the forts in defence of the country, they were left to the mercy and care of their slaves, to wade through rapid rivers, exposed to the inclemency of the weather, which happened then to be rainy; and in their way to a place of safety, encountering such difficulties as were hard to be endured by the sex. Their distresses were truly affecting, several of them died a short time after, from the fatigues they that day went through.

The militia in the town and suburbs of Roseau were soon in the field, to the number of not more than a hundred in the whole; few of the French inhabitants assembling at the first, and those that made their appearance soon after withdrew themselves, and were no more seen, till after the island was surrendered. The militia were distributed among the different forts in and above the town; where,

with

with the assistance of the few soldiers, some of whom were of the artillery, they greatly incommoded the enemy while landing at point Michael, by firing from all the batteries which they occupied.

These were, however, in a very bad state; the gun-carriages were all rotten, so that after two or three discharges the wheels were broken to pieces. The cannon in Melville's battery especially, where the most execution was done, being in that situation, were afterwards obliged to be laid on the parapets, there loaded, and fired off. Besides, in this fort they were obliged to load the cannon with loose powder, there being none of it made up into cartridges; and the cartridges that were used there were fetched by the militia from fort Young, which is upwards of half a mile distant from the other. Nevertheless, what with the firing from this fort, and from two field-pieces on a point of land just under it, the French troops were

were greatly retarded when they endeavoured to attack Roseau, and upwards of forty of them were killed.

About noon the same morning, the whole of the enemy were landed, and pushed on their march for the town; when, having taken possession of the fort at Loubiere, which is adjoining thereto, they made several attempts to enter Roseau, but were as often driven back, by the very heavy firing then kept up from all the batteries.

Three times they were driven out of the fort at Loubiere, and twice when their colours were hoisted therein, the flag-staves were shattered to pieces by the balls from Melville's battery: their Commissary-general was killed there, and the Marquis de Bouillé very narrowly escaped sharing the same fate, by the pieces of the flag-staves, which tore away the couteau from his side.

This

This severe cannonading so greatly intimidated the French, that they evacuated the fort they had taken with much precipitation, and retreated to the side of a hill just opposite to it, out of the line of fire. There they remained a considerable time, as if to meditate on some other mode of attack; but shortly after, about two thousand of them gained possession of the heights above Roseau, where they seemed to wait the coming on of night, to make their further approaches.

This last circumstance determined the fate of the island; as the Lieutenant-governor, seeing the danger to which the small force he had would inevitably be exposed by a further resistance, he, with the advice of his Privy-council, then assembled at the Government-house, sent out a Flag of Truce to the Marquis de Bouillé, with offers to surrender the island by capitulation.

This offer was readily accepted, and the Marquis, under protection of the Truce, came with it to the Government-houfe, in order to grant his terms, and to fign his part of the Articles of Capitulation. While this was doing, the firing from the batteries ceafed, which gave two French frigates an opportunity of coming abreaft of Rofeau; when the Commanders of them, it is probable, not knowing that the ifland had furrendered, feeing the Englifh colours ftill flying, with thofe of the French under them on the fame ftaff, they fired fome broadfides into the town.

This unexpected falute exafperating the militia, they immediately returned it with a forty-two pound cannon-ball, which, however, fell wide of its mark, the gun, in the hurry they were in to fhew their refentment at fo flagrant a breach, as they fuppofed, of the Truce, being ill-pointed. This the militia were foon ready to rectify, by pointing
another

another gun of the same metal point blank on one of the frigates, to which it would, doubtless, have done considerable damage; but just as the match was going to be put to the touch-hole, the Marquis, with the Lieutenant-governor, came running into the fort, and begged them to desist; at the same time, hailing the frigates from the ramparts, acquainted their Commanders with the surrender of the place.

Matters being thus accommodated, the two Commanders in Chief returned to the Government-house, where the Articles of Capitulation being ready, were, by both of them, duly signed and concluded. This being done, the Marquis returned to his troops; and soon after marched them into Roseau, thereby taking possession of the country for his most Christian Majesty.

It is worth while noticing here, the ceremonies used on this occasion, as it is to be hoped they may never again happen in Dominica. The French troops marched into the town in most regular and solemn order, the drums beating a slow march, and the French soldiers, with small boughs and flowers in their hats by way of laurels, with assumed fierce countenances as they came by our small force, seemed to threaten it with instant dissolution. The English soldiers and inhabitants, with two field pieces in their front, and lighted matches, their muskets grounded, and standing in two divisions, the regulars on the right, the militia on the left. The latter were permitted to take up their arms, and to retire with them to their houses, amidst an almost lawless troop of ruffians, by whom they had to pass; and who, with curses and reproaches for being disappointed of plundering and murdering the inhabitants, still threatened them, if they were not satisfied. The
English

English soldiers left their arms grounded, and retired to a place appointed for them by the Lieutenant-governor; and the next day were sent off the island, agreeably to the Articles of Capitulation, which are as follows:

ARTICLES OF CAPITULATION,

Between the Marquis de Bouillé, General of the Windward West India Islands, belonging to his most Christian Majesty, and Governor Stuart, Commander in Chief, and the Inhabitants of the Island of Dominica, belonging to his Britannic Majesty.

ARTICLE I.

THAT we the Governor, chief officers, officers of the troops, and soldiers, shall go out with one mortar, two brass field pieces, and ten charges for each piece, with arms, baggage, and all the honours of war.

Granted,

Granted, that the garrison go out with all the honours of war; but afterwards to ground their arms, except the officers.

ARTICLE II.

That the regular troops, consisting of six officers and ninety-four men, including non-commissioned officers, soldiers, and cannoniers, be transported to England, by the shortest route, in a good vessel, with victuals for the voyage, or remain here on their parole.

Granted, on condition that they serve not against the King of France till they are exchanged; the officers to remain here on their parole, but not the soldiers.

ARTICLE III.

That the officers and others shall have liberty to take with them their wives and children to the English islands by the shortest route;

route; and that they shall be provided with a good vessel, and victuals for the voyage.

Granted.

ARTICLE IV.

The inhabitants of the island shall retire from their posts with all the honours of war, that is to say, with two brass field pieces, their arms and baggage, colours flying, drums beating, and lighted match.

Granted.

ARTICLE V.

The inhabitants of the island shall retain their civil government, laws, customs, and ordinances; justice shall be administered by the same persons who are now in actual charge thereof: and as to what regards the interior policy of the island, it is to be arranged between his most Christian Majesty's Governor and the

the inhabitants: and in case the island shall be ceded to the King of France at the peace, the inhabitants shall have their choice, to keep their own political government, or to accept that established in Martinique and the other French islands.

Granted, till the peace.

ARTICLE VI.

The inhabitants and their religious ministers shall be maintained in the possession of their estates, enjoy their possessions, moveable and immoveable, of what nature soever they may be; they shall be maintained and conserved in their privileges, rights, honours, and exemptions; and the free negroes and mulattos in their liberties.

Granted.

ARTICLE VII.

They shall pay no other duties to his most Christian Majesty, than what they paid to his Britannic Majesty, nor other duties or imposts. The expences for administration of justice, the salaries of ministers, and other ordinary expences, to be paid out of the revenues of his most Christian Majesty, as during the government of his Britannic Majesty.

Granted; but the inhabitants of Dominica, for the liberty of exporting their produce, must pay the office of the Domains the same duties that the inhabitants pay in the French islands, or in Europe; but the expences for administration of justice are to be paid by the colony.

ARTICLE VIII.

The slaves, baggage, merchandize, and all other things made prizes of during the attack of the island, shall be restored.

Granted; they shall be faithfully restored.

ARTICLE IX.

The inhabitants who are absent, and those in the service of his Britannic Majesty, shall be maintained in their possessions, and enjoy their goods, by virtue of their proper attornies.

Granted.

ARTICLE X.

The inhabitants shall not be obliged to furnish lodgings, or any other matters, for the troops, nor slaves to work on the fortifications.

There are cases of necessity that will admit of no exceptions; but in common cases the troops shall be lodged at the expence of the King, in the houses which belong to him.

ARTICLE XI.

The ships, brigs, schooners, and other vessels, belonging to the inhabitants of the island, shall remain the property of their owners.

Granted; but English vessels from Europe shall be delivered up with fidelity to the King's navy.

ARTICLE XII.

The widows and other inhabitants, who, by sickness, absence, or other obstacles, are prevented from signing the Capitulation at present, shall have a limited time allowed them for doing the same.

Granted.

ARTICLE XIII.

The inhabitants and merchants of the island, who are comprized in this present Capitulation, shall enjoy all the privileges of commerce, on the same conditions as are allowed to the subjects of his most Christian Majesty in all his dominions.

Granted.

ARTICLE XIV.

The inhabitants shall enjoy their religion, and their ministers shall enjoy their cures.

Granted.

ARTICLE XV.

The inhabitants shall observe a strict neutrality, and shall not be forced to take up arms against his Britannic Majesty, nor against any other power,

Granted;

Granted; but the French-born subjects shall be at liberty to serve the King of France; and in case Dominica should return to the power of England, those who do not chuse to serve, shall not be punished by the French government.

ARTICLE XVI.

All the prisoners taken during the attack of the island shall be restored.

Granted.

ARTICLE XVII.

The merchants of the island may receive any vessels, that shall be addressed to them, from any part of the world, without being liable to confiscation,—dispose of their merchandize, and carry on their commerce; and the port shall be free for that purpose, they paying the ordinary duties paid in the French islands.

Granted,

Granted, till the peace, English vessels only excepted.

ARTICLE XVIII.

The inhabitants shall keep their arms.

Granted, on condition that they serve not against the King of France.

ARTICLE XIX.

That none other, except the actual residents of the island, shall be possessed of houses or lands, by purchase, or otherwise, till the peace; but after the peace, in case the island shall be ceded to the King of France, such inhabitants as do not chuse to live under the French government, shall be at liberty to dispose of their possessions and goods, moveable and immoveable, to whom they please, and to retire where they think proper; for which purpose they shall have a reasonable time allowed them.

Granted.

ARTICLE XX.

The inhabitants of the island may send their children to England to receive their education, to return hither, and to be supplied with necessaries during their stay in England.

Granted.

ARTICLE XXI.

The inhabitants may dispose of their goods and possessions to whom they think proper.

Granted.

ARTICLE XXII.

That the Court of Chancery shall be held by the Members of the Council, in the same form it is at present; and that appeals from the said Court shall be made of course in England, in the same manner as heretofore.

Granted.

ARTICLE XXIII.

That the wives of the officers and others, on leaving the island, may retire with their effects, and a number of domestics suitable to their rank.

Granted.

ARTICLE XXIV.

The persons belonging to privateers, and those who have no property in the island, who do not chuse to remain in it, shall have a vessel to carry them to the English islands, and be furnished with provisions for the voyage.

Granted, during the space of six weeks.

ARTICLE XXV.

DEMANDED BY THE FRENCH GENERAL.

There shall be delivered up to the General of the French troops, all the artillery and
other

other effects in the colony, belonging to the King of England; all the batteries on the coasts shall be restored to the same state they were in before the attack of the island; all the small arms, which belong to the King of England, shall be restored, except those of the officers and militia; no powder shall be taken from the magazines; they shall be delivered into the hands of such persons as shall be appointed by the Marquis de Bouillé.

Granted, by Governor Stuart; the preceding Articles being granted by the Marquis de Bouillé.

ARTICLE XXVI.

DEMANDED BY THE FRENCH GENERAL.

The magazines of provisions, and other effects, belonging to the King of England, shall be delivered up to the Commissary employed in the colony.

Granted by Governor Stuart.

ARTICLE XXVII.

OTHER ARTICLE DEMANDED BY THE FRENCH GENERAL.

Governor Stuart shall deliver up to-morrow, the 8th of September, 1778, the posts at Prince Rupert's Bay, after the Capitulation is signed. Fort Young shall be delivered directly into the hands of the first company of grenadiers; the forts and batteries of the town shall be delivered up at the same time, and all other fortresses of the colony, as soon as it possibly can be done.

Granted by Governor Stuart.

We the Governor-general of the French Windward islands in America, for his most Christian Majesty the King of France; and the Lieutenant-governor and Commander in Chief of Dominica, for his Britannic Majesty, the King of England, do ratify these Articles of of Capitulation in twenty-seven Articles as above, and oblige ourselves reciprocally to abide by the same.

Done in two parts at Roseau, Dominica, Signed and sealed with our seals at arms; and countersigned by our Secretaries, this 7th day of September, 1778,

(Signed)
De Bouillé and *William Stuart*.
And underneath by the General *Doublé*,
And by the Lieut. Governor *Hawkes*.

CHAPTER VIII.

OF THE GOVERNMENT OF THE ISLAND UNDER THE FRENCH, WITH A RELATION OF THE DISTRESSED SITUATION OF THE ENGLISH INHABITANTS, UNTIL ITS RESTORATION TO GREAT BRITAIN; TOGETHER WITH THE ACCOUNT OF THAT EVENT, AND SEVERAL OTHER SUBJECTS.

THUS fell the important island of Dominica into the hands of the French; and with it were lost all those advantages, that it was afterwards discovered would have accrued to the English, had it been in their possession during the last war.

This island, from its local situation, being exactly between the two principal islands of the French, Martinique and Guadeloupe, is the best calculated of all the possessions of Great Britain in that part of the world, to secure her the dominion of those seas. Had a few ships

ships of war been stationed at Prince Rupert's bay, they would have effectually stopped all intercourse of the French settlements with each other; as not a vessel could have passed or repassed, but would have been liable to capture by the British cruizers off that bay, and to windward of the island.

The island of Saint Lucia, that burying-place of thousands of brave Englishmen, would then, it is probable, have remained in the desolate state it was in before its surrender, as of no importance to the French. And it is most certain, that had Dominica been retained, at half the expence of men and money which it cost Great Britain to reduce the other, the loss of most of the English settlements in the West Indies would have been prevented, and the French would then have had sufficient employment in securing their own.

The importance of this island to the English was so well known, and dreaded by the French at that time, that the taking it out of our possession was the first object in their attack on the British settlements: and the Marquis de Bouillé actually secured Dominica for his nation, before hostilities between the two Crowns were known in the English West Indies.

The forces under the command of the Marquis, on this expedition, consisted of near three thousand regular troops, and near half that number of volunteers, composed of white men, mulattos, and negros. The naval armament consisted of three frigates, one a forty-gun ship, and upwards of thirty sail of armed sloops and schooners.

For several days after the surrender, the inhabitants from all parts of the island came to the Government-house, in order to sign the

Articles of Capitulation. During the time, some of the English inhabitants were accused to the Marquis, by some of the French, with having fitted out privateers against the Americans. These persons were treated with great indignity by the Marquis, who obliged them to pay down considerable sums of money for vessels said to have been French property, which had been captured as Americans by the privateers.

The principal accusers of the English inhabitants, on this and several other occasions, were certain French people, who had, heretofore, been treated with every indulgence and kindness by those they accused; as they were also the chief promoters of all the disturbances, heart-burnings, and animosities of the French government, to the British inhabitants of the island, during the whole of the time it was in their possession; and were, moreover, the means of obliging several to quit it, leaving behind them their property.

These were Thomas C——d A———t, W———m R———d, and a M———r C———r. The latter had formerly dealt largely with some English merchants of the island, whom he had defrauded of their dues by running away; but returning on this expedition, as chief guide to the troops, he was promoted by the Marquis de Bouillé to the office of chief baker to the forces in the place, as a reward of his treachery. R———d had quitted that country in the same clandestine manner; but returning with the Marquis, as a volunteer in the cause, was by him appointed his most Christian Majesty's Receiver-general of Dominica. C———d A———t had been a number of years a trustee for the French church-lands in Roseau, to which office he was appointed by the English government, at the time of the cession of the country to Great Britain.

Britain. He had, moreover, been treated with a degree of indulgence in his office, more than his behaviour entitled him to, and which he repaid, by taking every step in his power to do injury to the English inhabitants of the island after its surrender to the French.

The fate of these three men is worth remarking, as the recital may serve to deter others from being guilty of the like treacherous and mischievous doings. The Baker, whose infamous character soon came to the knowledge of the French government, was discharged from that office for fraud in his weights, and again obliged to fly the country. The Receiver-general, after having exercised his new office with every species of imposition and insolence in a degree peculiar to himself, very prudently took a silent departure from the island, a few days before its evacuation by the French, as being conscious
of

of his meriting a juft punifhment had he remained. And C———d A———t, as foon as the ifland was reftored, retired on his plantation in the country; where, univerfally detefted by both French and Englifh, he died of defpair but a fhort time after.

As foon as the new form of government was fettled by the Marquis de Bouillé, he departed for Martinique, leaving the Marquis Duchilleau Commander in Chief of his conqueft. This Governor had an univerfal antipathy to the Englifh, the very name of an Englifhman being hateful to his ears; nor could he bear them in his fight with any degree of temper; and contrary to the character of men in general of his nation, he extended his brutal behaviour even to the female fex, if they came in his way, to petition or addrefs him in behalf of their property.

Withal,

Withal, he was so very pusillanimous, that the most vague report of the approach of the English from Saint Lucia terrified him; when, galloping up and down like a madman, he would threaten every Englishman he met, to put them to death, and to set fire to the town, should their countrymen dare to attempt an invasion. And moreover, not confiding in the great number of troops that were under his command, but thinking them not sufficient to quell an insurrection of the English inhabitants, whom he weakly supposed might make an attempt to retake the island, he thought proper to break through the eighteenth Article of the Capitulation, by disarming them, and distributing their arms among the runaway negros, with whom he actually entered into a treaty for assistance.

This was the Governor whom the Marquis de Bouillé, from motives of policy, thought fit to appoint over his first conquest; and there could not have been a more proper perſon for carrying the intentions of the Marquis into execution, by leſſening the value of Dominica, in order to have it ceded to the French at the concluſion of the war. In this, however, happily for the Britiſh nation, he was diſappointed; and although the greateſt part of the Engliſh inhabitants, from the harſh and cruel treatment they underwent, not only from the Marquis Duchilleau, but alſo from every French perſon in office under his government, was driven to the neceſſity of quitting the iſland; yet the few that remained, patiently enduring all their ſufferings from the French, waited only the commencement of peace, to determine whether the country would be reſtored to the Engliſh, or be continued under the dominion of France. The former happening to be the caſe, was a matter of great concern to the French, who, well knowing its importance, quitted their poſſeſſions with the greateſt reluctancy, from a conviction

tion that it was an island capable of being rendered both formidable and dangerous to their own settlements at a future period.

To return to the Marquis Duchilleau; he, like another tyrannic governor, issued a proclamation, forbidding the assembling together of the English inhabitants more than two in a place. That no lights were to be seen in their houses after nine o'clock at night; that no English person was to be out after that hour, in the streets, without a candle and lanthorn, or a lighted pipe in his mouth; and that no servant of theirs was to be seen at night, without a ticket from his master; under no less a penalty to white-people, than being shot by the centinel at the post they passed by, of being imprisoned, or sent out of the island; and the servants were to be whipped in the public market, besides a fine on their masters.

Many of the English inhabitants were imprisoned by him on the slightest pretence; and one of them, Robert Thou, was actually shot by a centinel, for attempting to go on board his own vessel after nine o'clock at night. This unfortunate young man died a few days after, in the utmost torture from his wound, the ball going through his body at the breast; and the perpetrator of this horrid murder was raised by the Marquis Duchilleau to a higher station in his regiment, for having thus wantonly killed him.

So very apprehensive was this Governor, that the English inhabitants were forming designs to retake the island, or that they held a correspondence with the enemy at Saint Lucia, that every letter of theirs was opened for his inspection before it was delivered. And deeming this insufficient to come at the knowledge of their private transactions, he adopted the practice of going himself in disguise, or employing

ploying others, who better knew the English language, to listen at their doors and windows in the night-time; but luckily he never found out any secrets.

He repeatedly threatened to set fire to the town of Roseau, in case the island was attacked; and though the latter was never attempted by the English forces, yet that town was set fire to by the French soldiers, who, there is every reason to suppose, did it by his private orders. This supposition was strongly corroborated, by his behaviour on the night of that melancholy event, at which himself was present best part of the time; but he would not suffer his soldiers to assist in extinguishing the flames, save only in houses that belonged to the French inhabitants; especially in that of Thomas Chabaud Arnault, which, though several times on fire, was yet saved by the troops, in preference to far more valuable buildings

buildings that were confumed, while they ftood looking on, diverted with the fcene.

The foldiers were bufy, the chief time of the fire, in fecuring for themfelves the property of the inhabitants; breaking open boxes, trunks, and chefts, driving in the heads of cafks of liquor, and taking out what quantity they could in their hats, bottles, and other veffels, letting the reft run out into the ftreets. Some of the French inhabitants were alfo bufily employed in the fame manner; one of them in particular, of the name of " P———n," was actually detected with feveral articles of value belonging to Englifh people; and in particular a cafk of Madeira wine, the property of a Mr. John Tileftone, a reputable tavern-keeper in that town; who afterwards recovered the value of it by a fuit at law againft the faid P———n.

This

This fire in Roseau happened the evening of Easter Sunday, 1781, by which upwards of five hundred houses were consumed in a few hours; and among them the principal buildings, stores, a vast quantity of rich merchandize, and valuable articlesof houshold goods were destroyed, to the amount of upwards of two hundred thousand pounds sterling.

The inferior French officers, and several of the French inhabitants of Dominica, encouraged thereto by the tyrannic behaviour of the Marquis Duchilleau, were not backward in their bad treatment of the English inhabitants: the officers usually insulting them as they walked the streets; throwing showers of stones on their houses in the night-time; saluting the English white women with indecent expressions as they passed by; taking the upper hand of the men in taverns, and other places of necessary resort, where they happened to be present, or indignantly driving them out; circumstances of such mean cruelty to a conquered people, that one should think, none but the dregs of mankind would ever be guilty of.

This too was the behaviour of some of the French inhabitants; from whom it was, in a particular manner, distressing to the English, who had heretofore treated them with every degree of kindness, as being a set of people, who, though not of the same nation by birth, were members of the same community, subject to the same government, and as such, entitled to the same privileges and respect with themselves. Of these in particular, a Frenchman of colour, of the name of Blanchdelablong, and a white man, named Etienne Vring, deserve to be mentioned. The first had the audacity to strike the English Chief Justice, and the other insolently drew his sword on a respectable English merchant in a public tavern.

It is, however, necessary here to do justice to the merits of some of the principal French officers at that time; as of the Count de Bourgoinne, Monsieur du Beaupé, and the generality of the officers of Irish Brigades in that island.

The Count de Bourgoinne was Chief Governor of Dominica for some time after the Marquis Duchilleau had quitted it, to assist in the expedition formed by the French and Spaniards against Jamaica; and during the time of his government, the English inhabitants were much better treated, than while under Duchilleau. But this not answering the politic views of the Marquis de Bouillé, he recalled the Count from his government, under pretence of his mal-administration; but in reality, only for his lenity to the English inhabitants of Dominica.

Monsieur du Beaupé succeeded this latter; and although he was no great admirer of the English, yet, during his government, which lasted till the island was restored, the inhabitants of that description enjoyed some little repose from their sufferings, as he made it a point to prevent their being mal-treated by those under his command.

The Irish officers of the Brigades being acquainted with the customs, and speaking the language of the English, treated them with every civility in their power, during the time they were in the island; frequently visiting them, joining them on parties of amusement, and rendering them several little services. And to their praise be it mentioned, that on two or three occasions some of them opposed the
French

French officers, for their bad treatment of the English, at the risk of losing their own lives.

During five years and a quarter, the time that the island of Dominica was in possession of the French, it was resorted to by no vessels from Old France; nor was any of the produce of the English plantations exported to that kingdom during this period; but part of it was sent in neutral bottoms to the Dutch island of Saint Eustatius, before its capture by Admiral Rodney; and from thence it was exported to England, under the most extravagant expences and loss to the proprietors.

Other parts of the produce were sent in Dutch vessels, which were engaged for the purpose in England, to Rotterdam, where, on their arrival, the sugar in particular sold from sixteen to eighteen pounds sterling per hogshead.

After

After the breaking out of the war with the Dutch, the produce of Dominica was sent, under Imperial colours, to Ostend, where the sugar sold only from six to eight pounds sterling per hogshead. This was a great falling off in the price of that commodity, and greatly distressed the sugar planters in particular; but to complete their misfortunes, one of those very vessels, laden with returns to the island, was captured by the Americans, who sold both the ship and cargo.

The prices of the different articles in Dominica, the greatest part of the time of the French government of it, were as follow:

Sugar, from 1l. 4s. to 1l. 10s. per Cwt.
Rum, 2s. per gallon.
Coffee, from 2l. to 2l. 10s. per Cwt.

Of the current money of the island, which was at eighty-five per cent. and was not more than one-half the value of the same produce at present. The freight of shipping it off from the out-bays to Roseau, was then nearly double to what it is now; and the duties paid to the French Custom-house, for exporting the sugar alone, was upwards of twenty per cent. on their estimation of its value.

The different articles of provisions, and other necessaries, brought to the island, were at a most extravagant price.

Beef, from 9l. 18s. to 11l. 5s. per barrel.
Pork, from 11l. 5s. to 13l. 4s. per ditto.
Flour, from 9l. 18s. to 12l. per ditto.
Butter, from 10l. to 13l. 4s. per firkin.

This was the wholesale price; but when disposed of again at retail, the price was extravagant; for butter was not to be had there under six shillings a pound, candles

dles at three shillings, soap at the same price, and every other article in that advanced proportion.

The English inhabitants then of Dominica were, in consequence, greatly distressed; as few of them could afford to purchase those necessary articles, the planters, and lower order of people especially; the latter having no trade, and but little to do, were unable to be at so great an expence; and the planters having a number of negros on their estates, were distressed to furnish a necessary supply of provisions for their slaves, or for themselves.

Many were under the necessity of purchasing from the French soldiers their allowance from the King, of salt meat, bread, and other matters; which, though not the best provisions of the kind, were a great assistance to a number

ber of the inhabitants, as well in the towns as on the plantations.

On the other hand, the island of Saint Lucia, soon after its capture by the English, was rendered a place far more desirable, in point of trade, than it had ever been, while under its former masters; and the French inhabitants of it were better treated by the English government, officers and soldiers, than they actually treated their own countrymen, who retired thither after its surrender.

That island was the chief mart of trade for provisions and merchandize of every description, during the war, being resorted to by vessels, not only from our own settlements, but also from most of the foreign islands, by the means of flags of truce. Provisions in particular, were to be had there at the following moderate prices, viz.

Beef,

Beef, from 5l. 10s. to 6l. per barrel.
Pork, from 6l. 10s. to 7l. per ditto.
Flour, from 3l. 6s. to 4l. per ditto.
Butter, from 4l. 10s. to 5l. per firkin.

Although the French government of Dominica had every opportunity of furnishing their troops with fresh provisions, by means of the Americans, then in alliance with France, yet not a single vessel arrived there with cattle, during the whole time they were in possession of the island. But the cattle that were killed for the use of the troops were, at first, indiscriminately shot on the English plantations, at the pleasure of Duchilleau, whenever they were wanted for the use of his soldiers.

He afterwards established an ordinance, that every English planter should send a beast in his turn for the use of the military hospital, under the penalty of having it taken by force;

and

and the person who did not comply, was imprisoned, or sent off the island. By this means, upwards of sixty in every hundred head of cattle in the country were destroyed during his Government; and this ordinance was carried into execution with such rigour by him, that if either by detention, by bad weather, or delay, by reason of the distance of the estate from Roseau, the cattle were not there in time, a party of soldiers, with their muskets loaded, were immediately sent out, to kill any horned beast that fell in their way.

By this arbitrary proceeding, many fine milch cows of the inhabitants in the town fell victims to his wrath on these occasions; and what was particularly hard upon the owners of them, they were obliged to bear the loss without repining, and to put up with being paid as for ordinary beasts, and waiting for that payment a long time.

Another very great hardship on the owners of cattle, killed for the use of the military hospital, was, that they were seldom permitted to have a piece for themselves, though they paid for it, but were obliged to be satisfied with the offals of the carcase. And, as for others of the English, a piece of bullock's liver was the most they in general could get; and they were usually told by the French officers in the markets, " That that " was too good for an Englishman."

This great destruction of the cattle in Dominica, at that time, was a source of great disadvantages to the proprietors of the sugar plantations, thereby preventing the possibility of carrying on the culture of the sugar-cane, from the want of those necessary animals. And by this procedure of the French, several of the English planters were driven to the necessity of stopping the further settlement of their estates, to the great detriment of themselves

selves and families, as well as injury to the mortgagees in Europe; and at the same time, lessening the value of property in the island in the opinion of people in general.

The French were satisfied with being able to keep the country from Great Britain during the war, firmly believing, that it would be ceded to them at the peace; they did, therefore, every thing in their power to render the stay of the English inhabitants uncomfortable and distressing. Their disappointment, therefore, on finding the island was to be restored, was matter of great concern to them; and they actually put off the delivering it up to the English, a considerable time after the ratification of the definitive treaty of peace was concluded in Europe.

Some weeks before the actual restoration of Dominica, an English regiment from Saint Lucia arrived at Roseau, for the purpose of taking poffeffion of the ifland for his Britannic Majefty. This was, however, peremptorily refufed by the French Governor, who ftrongly denied his having received any inftructions for the delivering up the ifland from his fuperiors at Martinique, or even from Europe; at the fame time, ordering the Britifh Commander, with his troops, to depart, and threatening to compel them to it. But this order being contrary to the commiffion of the latter, he declared he was determined to act as became him; in confequence of which, he was at laft permitted to land with his troops at point Michael, there to wait till the French Governor had further inftructions.

Matters being thus accommodated, owing, it is probable, to the fuperior force of the Englifh, who came with two fhips of war to demand the ifland, which was then but thinly garrifoned; the Englifh troops were accordingly landed at the before-mentioned place,
where

where they continued till the day of the surrender of the country to Great Britain.

It is worth while to remark here, the jealous behaviour of the French Commander on this occasion; for though there was every reason to believe, that he well knew the island was to be restored; yet he took every method that was in his power of shewing a disposition to prevent it; and he actually threatened to use force if the English dared to land, as if upon an hostile occasion: nor would he permit any of the English officers so much as to set their feet on shore in Roseau; but lined the bay of that road with armed soldiers, who even then treated some of the English inhabitants exceedingly ill, for no other reason, than the joy that was visible in their faces at the sight of their own countrymen.

This assumed face of resistance, was a plain indication of the great unwillingness of the

French to quit possession of the country; but which would have little availed them, had the English Commander been disposed to force his landing. This, however, would have been productive of fatal consequences to the defenceless English inhabitants, who would, there is no doubt, have fallen victims to the fury of the French in the first instance, and it would have answered no other end, than to facilitate the return of the island to its former government a few weeks sooner.

The English inhabitants soon after made themselves amends, for having been prevented from saluting their countrymen on their arrival; for on the same evening there was scarcely a man, woman, or child, in the town and suburbs of Roseau, that did not either ride or walk to the quarters of the English troops at point Michael, for the purpose of rejoicing at the prospect of a speedy return of their own government.

One

One obfervation is due to the fpirited behaviour of the Britifh Commander while at point Michael; he caufed it to be well fortified and guarded, for fear of the worft, and every day hoifted the Englifh flag. This being a moft hateful fight to the French, their Commander repeatedly fent orders to have the Englifh colours taken down, which the other as peremptorily refufed; alledging, that this country was his mafter's, whofe flag he would defend to the laft moment of his life; and that if the French Governor would have it down, he muft enforce his commands with the muzzles of his guns.

From this time, till the evacuation of Dominica, the French were bufily employed in demolifhing the fortifications they had built, and doing all the damage they could to thofe that were there before their invafion, feveral of which they blew up with gunpowder.

This island was restored to England in the month of January, 1783. The day of its restoration was a joyful day for the English inhabitants, especially for those who had undergone a long and painful captivity, and had been treated with a degree of cruelty hardly to be paralleled.

In the morning of the day of the evacuation the English troops marched from point Michael; and between eleven and twelve o'clock they came near the town of Roseau, where, waiting till the French began to embark, it was near two o'clock before they finally evacuated the island; and then the English troops came into the town, with colours flying, drums beating, and a band of music playing as they marched, escorted by most of the English inhabitants, who, with multitudes of negros, lined both sides of the way as they entered the town.

Between

Between one and two o'clock, a company of the Train of Artillery took poffeffion of the principal fort in Rofeau, marching in, while the French troops marched out; and proceeded to the water-fide, where their boats being ready, they immediately embarked, amidft the hiffes and curfes of the Englifh inhabitants, whom they had heretofore fo cruelly treated.

As foon as the Britifh troops were in poffeffion of the fort, they hoifted the ftandard of England on the flag-ftaff, which being a fight few of the inhabitants had feen before, and being elated with joy on the occafion, they were fo eager to lend their affiftance to hoift it, that they were nearly pulling the halliards, by which it was raifed, to pieces, and breaking down the flag-ftaff by the force of their numbers. The fight of the Britifh ftandard was alfo a matter of great admiration to the French, who, it is probable, had never feen

one

one before; and they seemed to view it with no satisfaction, as they passed by it in their boats, probably, on comparing the beauties of it with the fading pale colour of their own.

Soon after the French were embarked, the new English Governor, John Orde, Esq. landed from a frigate in the bay, under a discharge of cannon from that vessel; which salute was returned by the fort on his landing. When escorted by the whole of the English inhabitants, amidst the shouts of " Long live " King George," he was conducted to the Court-house in Roseau; and after having had his commission proclaimed, and taking the usual oaths on the occasion, he retired to partake of the general joy, and of a very genteel entertainment prepared for him by the colony.

CHAPTER IX.

CONTAINS AN ACCOUNT OF THE DIVISION OF THE ISLAND INTO PARISHES AND TOWNS, WITH A DESCRIPTION OF ITS CAPITAL, THE PRINCIPAL BUILDINGS, FORTIFICATIONS, AND HARBOUR; TOGETHER WITH OBSERVATIONS ON PRINCE RUPERT'S BAY, AND THE GRAND SAVANNAH IN THAT ISLAND.

DOMINICA is divided into ten parishes, viz. Saint Mark's, Saint Luke's, Saint Paul's, Saint Peter's, Saint John's, Saint George's, Saint Andrew's, Saint David's, Saint Patrick's, and Saint Joseph's. In each of these parishes a spot of land is marked out for building a town on, which was appropriated to that purpose by the Commissioners on the first cession of the country to England; but few of them have more than two or three small mean houses on them, and therefore do not deserve further notice.

The

The town of Roseau is at present the capital of the island, and is situated in the parish of Saint George, being about seven leagues from Prince Rupert's Bay. It is on a point of land on the S.W. side of the island, which point of land forms two bays, viz. Woodbridge's Bay to the north, and Charlotte-ville Bay to the southward.

Roseau is about half a mile in length, from Charlotte-ville to Roseau river, and two furlongs in breadth, but less in some parts, being of a very irregular figure. It contains not more than five hundred houses, exclusive of a number of small wooden buildings, occupied by negros, which give it rather an unpleasing appearance from the sea.

The streets of this town are also very irregular, not one of them being in a straight line; but the whole of them form very acute angles, which face nearly the entrance of each

each other, and appear very incommodious and unsightly. They are, however, mostly well paved, are in general from forty to fifty feet wide, and the town is very pleasantly situated.

Previous to the capture of the island by the French, this town contained upwards of one thousand good houses; but the fire which happened there, as before-mentioned, consumed the major part of them; and the ruins still remain, as a memorial of that unfortunate event.

The public buildings in Roseau are, the Government-house, Court-house, Secretary's, Register's, and Provost Marshal's offices, the church, market-house, and gaol.

The Government-house is situated in Charlotte-ville, which joins to Roseau, or is rather the

the upper part of it, being included in the map of that town. It is a large building of wood, built after the French manner in the West Indies, two stories high, with galleries all round, and joiced. It stands in the middle of a large lot of ground, surrounded with a low stone wall, has a very fine garden at the back of it, and in front a long gravelly walk, very prettily ornamented on each side with cocoa-nut and other trees, which gives it a very rural appearance from the sea-side.

The Court-house is a neat wooden building, on the next lot of land to the Government-house to the southward. This building is two stories high, has a neat portico on pillars in front, and large open gallery backwards, the windows of it joiced. In the upper apartments are a large council-chamber, rooms for the juries, and a gallery for the spectators, or others having business at the courts. In the lower apartments are raised seats for the judges,
a place

a place enclosed for the lawyers and officers of the courts, jury boxes, and a bar for the prisoners. In this building all causes, civil and criminal, are tried; and all public business of the colony is there transacted by the Governor, Council, and Assembly of the island.

The public Secretary's, Register's, and Provost Marshal's offices, are two low stone buildings in the yard of the Court-house, and are covered with tiles. These buildings are in no other respect remarkable, than being very badly contrived, and no ways adapted to the purposes for which they were intended; the tiles being frequently blown off in the hurricane seasons, renders them damp, and an improper place for keeping public records.

The church is a large lofty building of wood, but it is at present much out of repair. It has a neat pulpit, reading desk, and a few pews; but neither altar-piece, hangings, baptismal font, belfry, nor bell. This, the only Protestant church in the island, is built on a large lot of ground, has a good churchyard of very deep and excellent black mould; but the yard is not enclosed. Adjoining to it is a fine lot of land, which was laid out in the plan of the town, and reserved by the Commissioners, for the purpose of building thereon a public school; but it is at present appropriated to a quite different use.

The market-house has been erected since the restoration of the island to the English, and is of wood, built on pillars of stone, between which are apartments for the butchers and fishermen, and the public stocks for confinement of disorderly white people and negros; and the middle passage is for the loaded fish canoes, that they may be drawn up out of the heat of the sun while the fish is selling. The upper part of this building
is

is divided into two apartments, one for the Clerk of the market, and the other for the ufe of the Town Wardens of Rofeau, who hold their meetings there when they tranfact the public bufinefs. It is alfo ufed as a guard-room for the militia, during the three days and nights of Chriftmas holidays (a ufelefs piece of ceremony, only putting people to unneceffary trouble and expence) and in times of actual need, as fire; or any danger which threatens that town.

It may not be improper here to take fome notice of the market-place, and market of Rofeau. The former is a large open fquare, nearly in the centre of the town, on the bay; it is paved, and well adapted to the purpofe for which it was defigned; but the market is very poorly fupplied in general with butchers meat. This is partly owing to the fcarcity of horned cattle, few being killed, unlefs they are brought from North America, which, however,

however, has, of late years, been seldom the case, on account of the difficulties to which American vessels are subject in their trading with this island, several of them having been repeatedly refused admittance into the port with only that loading.

This has often greatly distressed the inhabitants of Dominica, who having few cattle of their own, and these few being necessary for the service of their plantations, it would have been highly imprudent to have used them for the purpose of supplying the market; as it would have impoverished their estates of those useful animals, without the least probability of getting them replaced by purchasing others: for the Americans, from having been so often refused admittance to dispose of their cargos of cattle, took so great a disgust against the inhabitants of the country, that even when they have had permission to trade thither, they have actually refused.

Nor

Nor is the market of Roseau, in general, well supplied with poultry, owing to the very blameable neglect of the generality of the planters, in not raising a sufficient quantity of feathered stock on their estates, of which they are so very capable. It is, however, well supplied with excellent fish of most kinds peculiar to the West Indies; vegetables and fruit of almost every description are to be had there, in great abundance, much cheaper and better than in most of the other islands.

Sunday is the chief market day there, as it is in all the West Indies; on this day the market is like a large fair, the negros from the plantations, within eight miles of Roseau, come thither in great numbers, each one bringing something or other to dispose of for himself, often to the amount of three or four dollars; and many of them, who bring kids, pigs, or fowls, seldom return home

home without fifty or sixty shillings, the produce of their articles.

The price of butchers meat is there very high, being as follows, viz.

	s.	d.	
Beef	1	1½	per pound.
Mutton	1	6	per ditto.
Veal	2	3	per ditto.
Goats flesh	1	1½	per ditto.
Pork	0	10½	per ditto.

There is no established price there for poultry, which, though sometimes tolerably plenty, especially on the plantations of the French inhabitants, who chiefly send that article to market, is still excessive dear. A full-grown turkey will cost from 16s. 6d. to 24s. 9d. and often 30s. a goose at the same rate; a duck from 6s. to 9s. and a dunghill fowl at the same extravagant price.

The wild game of the woods, as pigeons, doves, and partridges, which, though at times, in the seasons for killing them, are very plentiful, yet bear a most extravagant price; a wild pigeon will cost 3s. a dove or partridge 1s. 6d. and other small birds of the country are at a very high rate. This is entirely owing to the want of laws for regulating the prices of those necessary articles in the island; as those who make a trade of them have the liberty of fixing what price they please; thereby being guilty of great extortion, to the sensible inconvenience of the inhabitants.

Eggs and milk are tolerably reasonable, and the latter is in general very good; but those who chiefly supply the market with it, adulterate it.

Notwithstanding fish of all sorts are caught in great plenty in all the bays of the island, yet that article bears a much higher price in Dominica, than in moſt other Engliſh ſettlements. This is alſo owing to the want of proper regulations in the fiſh market; for though there is an act for obliging every fiſherman, who catches fiſh within a certain diſtance from Roſeau, to bring it there for ſale, yet the major part of the inhabitants, who are Roman Catholics, faſt the greateſt part of the week upon fiſh; and the fiſhermen, being all of the ſame religion, they contrive to evade this act, by ſending the beſt part of their fiſh to their friends, and bring only what they cannot otherways diſpoſe of to the market. By this means that article is often ſcarce, as well as dear; and on particular faſt days, in Lent eſpecially, the Engliſh inhabitants are frequently obliged to faſt without fiſh.

It has often been wondered at, that in Dominica there are no Engliſh fiſhermen; and that a buſineſs, which is known to be ſo very

advan-

advantageous, should be entirely carried on only by the French inhabitants. This neglect of the English is the more remarkable, from the great inconveniences they labour under, from not having a fishery of their own; but though a thing of the kind was attempted by Mr. Beves, a respectable English inhabitant, in the time of the French government of the island, it failed, through the malice of some of the French inhabitants; and that no other Englishman, since the return of the country to its former government, has thought it worth while to repeat the trial, is a matter of much surprize.

The present price of fish in the market of Roseau is as follows, viz.

	s.	d.	
River fish	1	6	per pound.
Sea ditto, caught with hook and line	1	0	per ditto.
Seine and pot fish	0	4½	per ditto.
Turtle	1	6	per ditto.

This is certainly a very high price for that commodity; a pound of river fish, at 1s. 6d. current money, is 10d. sterling per pound, at eighty per cent. the present rate of exchange of money in that island; and hook and line fish, at 1s. is 6d. sterling and a fraction per pound, at the same rate of exchange, a price which greatly exceeds that of the same commodity in England, where it is not to be had in such great plenty as in Dominica, and by no means in so great perfection, especially in the city of London.

The public goal in Roseau has been erected since the restoration of the island to Great Britain, but it is not yet quite finished. It is of fine stone, erected in a very healthy situation, on a large lot of land, and the building on a large scale, is commodious, and well adapted to the design.

The

The expences of purchasing the land, and building a part of this gaol, were defrayed out of the money humanely contributed by several worthy persons in England, for the relief of the unfortunate sufferers by the fire in Roseau, in the year 1781, before noticed; but which money, after it was sent out to Dominica, could not be distributed to the persons for whom it was intended, owing to the deaths of some, and the removal of others from the island soon after that heavy calamity; the rest consented with the Governor, Council, and Assembly, to its being appropriated in that manner.

This building will be a lasting monument of the generous and praise-worthy endeavours of Englishmen, to alleviate the distresses of their fellow-subjects, in a country so far distant from themselves.

The road of Roseau, for it cannot properly be called an harbour, it being rather an open bay, is very capacious; and from Woodridge's bay, which joins it to the northward, to the bay of Charlotte-ville, contained the French and Spanish fleets, consisting of upwards of four hundred sail of men of war and transport ships, which lay at anchor for several days previous to their sailing on their intended attack of Jamaica last war, in 1782. This road is often dangerous in the hurricane months, and has frequently proved fatal to vessels, whose Commanders were so imprudent as to keep them there at anchor, from the end of August to October; during which time, almost every year, the sea very often tumbles into this road from the southward in a very frightful manner.

A very dreadful circumstance of this kind happened the last day of September, 1780; at which time the sea arose to the amazing
height

height of twenty-one feet perpendicular above its ufual furface, and its billows broke upwards of one hundred yards from the common fhore. It deftroyed feveral houfes in front of the beach, drove feveral fmall veffels from their anchors, and carried them up into the town; other veffels foundered, or were dafhed to pieces in the night-time; the dead bodies of the crews, with the pieces of the veffels, were driven on fhore, and the morning of next day exhibited the moft fhocking fpectacle of its unbounded fury.

The fortifications of Rofeau are, Young's Fort, Melville's Battery, Bruce's Hill Batteries, and Fort Demoullin.

Young's Fort is juft oppofite the Government-houfe, from the front wall of which it is feparated only by the highway. It is well mounted with cannon, has a powder magazine, an arfenal for fmall arms, and commodious

dious barracks for the officers and foldiers; but owing to its bad conſtruction, only two or three of the cannon in it will bear on any particular object; and it is, befides, entirely under command of all the other batteries of the town on the hills above it.

Melville's Battery, as before obferved, was the principal place from whence the moſt material fervice was done, in preventing the French from entering Rofeau on the 7th of September, 1778. This battery has fome very heavy cannon on it, but the works of it are all gone to decay, and it is at prefent wholly neglected.

Bruce's Hill, which is juſt above Rofeau, has feveral fine batteries, with one for mortars, commodious barracks, and feveral blockhoufes. It had a fine ſtone ciſtern in the time of the French, but which, being built by them, they thought proper to deſtroy and blew

blew it up, a few days before they evacuated the island, thereby rendering it useless. However, the aqueduct, by which it was supplied with water, has been since discovered, and is of great use to that fortification, which is, upon the whole, well calculated for the defence of the town, when attacked only from the sea; but being under the command of other heights above it, it would soon be rendered untenable, was it to be attacked on the land-side, as was the case the last war.

Demoullen's Hill fort is also well mounted with cannon, and is otherways well provided for the defence of the town; but it is subject to the same inconveniences as the other fortifications, being under the command of the heights above it.

These are the chief fortifications in Dominica at present, except that at Cashacrou, which

which is rather a signal post; the other batteries on the sea-coasts, at a distance from Roseau, being of small importance for the defence of the island, save only the works now raising at Prince Rupert's Bay.

This last is in the parish of Saint John, on the north-west part of the island, distant about seven leagues from the town of Roseau. The bay is three miles across, and one and a half deep, that is to say, from the extremity of each point, to the shore of the land laid out for a town. In this bay the whole of the British navy may safely ride at anchor all seasons of the year, and be well supplied with necessaries not be found at English harbours in Antigua, or any other part of the English West Indies, the rendezvous of the British fleet. It is surrounded by two high mountains, called the Cabrittes; the inner of which is about five hundred, and the outer six hundred feet perpendicular; both of them are out of the reach of other heights.

At

At the bottom of these mountains, between the inner one and the main land, is a large piece of swampy ground, upwards of one hundred acres in extent; which, if well drained, would pasture many cattle, sheep, and other stock, for the use of the garrison; and the stock, feeding under the muzzles of the guns, would be secure from being pillaged, or destroyed by the enemy.

Soon after the arrival of Colonel Andrew Fraser, his Majesty's chief Engineer for that island, the Legislature of Dominica, wishing to testify their readiness to co-operate with government, in the important work of fortifying Prince Rupert's Bay, well knowing that it would be the only effectual means of preserving the sovereignty of the country to Great Britain, they passed an act, granting to his Majesty the labour of one hundred negros, for three years, to be paid for by the colony.

The work was accordingly began, by cutting down the trees on the Cabrittes, tracing roads

roads to the tops of them, and draining the swamps; from which, in a few months, fifteen inches of water was carried off, and it was found that they could be effectually drained; whereby the healthiness of fort Shirley, which lays between the two Cabrittes, was established. But on the rumour of a fresh war, expected between England and France in 1787, the negros so granted by the colony were withdrawn from Prince Rupert's Bay by Governor Orde, who employed them on the fortifications of Roseau, particularly on Demoullen's Hill, the works of which were then first began. However, the fortifying the Cabrittes has since been re-commenced; and when completed, there is no doubt but that they will be nearly as formidable as the rock of Gibraltar.

At the distance of about twelve miles from Roseau, and nine miles from Prince Rupert's Bay, is the grand Savanna, which also might be be well fortified, and rendered of great service, for the defence of the island. The Savanna is a fine extensive plain, upwards of a mile in extent; is on a tolerable height above the sea-shore, and at a great distance from the mountains above it.

The occupying this place by the English, was strongly recommended to the then English Ministry by General Robert Melville, on the commencement of the last war with France; when, had it been adopted, there is every reason to believe, that Dominica would never have been attempted by the French; and it is probable, the reduction of all our other settlements, in that part of the world, would, by this means, have been prevented.

In the Savanna are large quarries of excellent free-stone, fit for every purpose of building. Of these, great quantities were sent by the French, while the island was in their possession, to their other settlements; to that of Guadeloup in particular, where some of their churches, and other capital structures, are wholly built of those stones.

CHAPTER X.

THE CIVIL GOVERNMENT, OFFICERS, COURTS, AND OTHER SUBJECTS RELATIVE TO THEM; ALSO A DESCRIPTION OF THE MILITIA OF THAT ISLAND.

ON the cession of Dominica to Great Britain in 1763, the government of the island was included in that of Grenada and the Grenadines, Saint Vincents, and Tobago, under General Robert Melville, but afterwards it was made a separate government under Sir William Young, in which independent state it remained till 1778, when the island was reduced by the French. Whilst they possessed the country, the government of it was the same as that of the other French windward islands; but after it was restored to England, it returned to its former independent government, and in that state it is at present.

The present establishment consists of a Governor and Commander in Chief, Lieutenant-governor, Council, Assembly, Magistrates, and Civil Officers.

The Chief Governor is the representative of the King, General of the forces, Vice Admiral, Chancellor, and Ordinary of the island. He grants all the militia commissions, and commissions for fitting out privateers; gives grants of land, renews the leases of the French inhabitants, or other leaseholders of the King; and also gives grants of poor settlers lots. He grants licences of marriage, licences to school-masters, and licences to tavern-keepers, or to sell spirituous liquors, to keep gaming tables, &c. &c. independent of the other parts of Legislature. His salary is two thousand pounds current money, which is paid him by the colony, exclusive of what he receives from the Crown; and also exclusive of his fees of office, which are very considerable.

The Lieutenant-governor is allowed no salary by the colony, but during the absence of the Commander in Chief, when he takes the supreme command, but receives only a moiety of the salary allowed by the colony to the former. In case of his death, or absence during that period, the chief command devolves to the senior Member of the Council, who then becomes Governor in Chief pro tempore, and enjoys the like salary as the Lieutenant-governor, during the time he acts in that capacity.

The Council consists of twelve Members, who are appointed by his Majesty's Writ of Privy Seal. Of these the Commander in Chief has the privilege to chuse seven, to be of his Privy-council; but the office of the whole is to assist him in the government, and to concur with the House of Assembly, in making and passing the laws, statutes, and ordinances of the colony.

The House of Assembly of Dominica consists of nineteen Members, who are the representatives of the people of the island, and are chosen by votes of the freeholders in each parish, in consequence of a writ issued for that purpose by the Commander in Chief, to the Provost Marshal of the place. Their office is, to prepare all public acts of the colony, which acts cannot be passed without their concurrence; to maintain the rights and privileges of their constituents, and to promote the happiness of the people of the country, as well as the interests of the Crown.

The Speaker of the Assembly's place is of great trust and respectability. Nine of the Members form a House, where they are attended by a Serjeant at Arms with the mace, who acts as Messenger, and who, with the Clerk of the Assembly, is paid a yearly salary by the colony.

The principal civil officers are, the Chief Juſtice, the Judge of the Court of Admiralty, King's Attorney-general, King's Solicitor-general, public Secretary, Regiſter, and Provoſt Marſhal.

The Chief Juſtice of Dominica is appointed by the Crown, and is a poſt of great honour and truſt. His courts are, Common Pleas, King's Bench, or Grand Seſſions of the Peace; at both of which he preſides as Chief Judge. He is alſo a Member of the Council, and an Aſſiſtant Juſtice of other Courts; his ſalary is ſix hundred pounds ſterling per annum, and his fees of office are very conſiderable.

The Judge of the Court of Admiralty for Dominica is alſo appointed by the Crown, but has no ſalary allowed him, his emoluments ariſing only from the condemnation of veſſels captured from the enemy, or ſuch as are ſeized by the Cuſtom-houſe for carrying on a clandeſtine

destine trade. He is also a Member of the Council, and Assistant Justice of the other Courts.

The King's Attorney-general, and the Solicitor-general, are both appointed by the Crown, and have each a salary allowed them. The public Secretary and Register, and the Provost Marshal enjoy their offices by patent; the latter acts as Usher of the Black Rod, and Messenger of the Council, the public Secretary as Clerk to that Board; they have a yearly salary allowed them by the colony.

There are, besides, Justices of the Quorum, who are all Members of the Council, Justices of the Peace, Coroner, Way-wardens, Town-wardens, and Constables in every parish of the island. The first three description of civil officers are appointed by commissions, under the Seal at Arms of the Governor in Chief;

the

the others are chosen in turn, every year, at the Court of Grand Sessions of the Peace.

The Courts of Dominica are, Court of Chancery, Ordinary, Vice Admiralty, King's Bench, Common Pleas, and Courts of Special Sessions. The first five are the same as those courts are in England, only that there may be appeals from them to those of the mother-country; and the Courts of Special Sessions are chiefly to try disorderly whites, or negroes guilty of capital crimes; and for fixing the standard of bread, meat, fish, and other articles of the markets. At these courts two or more Justices of the Peace preside, but one of them must be of the Quorum.

The fees of office in Dominica, as well as in all the English West India islands, are very high and burdensome on individuals, especially in some departments, where there are also other just causes of complaints; but which

it

it is not my intention to take notice of particularly at present. These excessive fees are peculiar to the British government in the West Indies, as it must, in justice to the French, be acknowledged, that there is no such thing among them; and that during the time they were in possession of Dominica last war, neither the French chief Governor, nor the other civil officers, received any fees from individuals for public business in their departments. Every thing was done gratis; and when they heard of a contrary practice under the English government, they expressed their disapprobation, as a practice not allowed by their government.

The militia of Dominica is at present only composed of foot, and includes all descriptions of white men, and free people of colour, from the age of eighteen to fifty years old, who are able to bear arms, and have resided thirty days at one time in the island.

A penalty

A penalty of six pounds twelve shillings is imposed on every one, who neglects or refuses to enlist himself within the time limited; which fine is doubled every field day after, until actual appearance. A penalty also of sixteen shillings and six-pence is laid for non-attendance in the field on field days, after being inrolled; and which is doubled every field day after, until the defaulter makes his appearance.

The field days were formerly the last Saturday in every month, but have been lately altered to the first Monday in each month; and sometimes, in cases of threatening danger, the militia meet every week, or oftener, at the discretion of the Legislature. The uniform of the militia infantry is, scarlet coats, with facings and cuffs of black velvet; that of the artillery, blue turned up with scarlet. These every person is obliged to furnish himself with; but
the

the arms, accoutrements, powder, flint, &c. are supplied by Government.

None are exempt from serving in the militia, except the Members of the Council, and the public Officers; but those who have borne commissions in the army, or in the militia, in other islands, are not liable to serve under the rank they were in before, unless it can be proved they have been broke for misbehaviour or cowardice.

The militia of Dominica, previous to the reduction of the island by the French, last war, were little inferior in discipline to regular troops, especially that part of them which was composed of English subjects. The defence they made on the 7th day of September, 1778, sufficiently convinced the Marquis de Bouillé that they merited that character, which he actually gave them in a very handsome compliment that day; but he at the same time expressed

pressed his astonishment, on seeing the smallness of their numbers, that they should have behaved so well, as to prevent him from subduing the island, as he had intended, without permitting it the benefit of a Capitulation.

The militia is, at present, in a very respectable state; but it would be much more so, was it to be composed only of English subjects; for the French and other foreigners, who are incorporated therein, from not understanding the words of command in English, or from a natural dislike to the service, pay no great attention to it; and in consequence very often throw the whole into disorder.

Here it may not be thought improper to observe, how very disagreeable this service is to the generality of the foreigners, who are inhabitants of this island; many of whom have repeatedly offered to pay a certain sum annually

to

to be wholly exempt from a duty which they cannot be induced to relish, unless under their own proper government. Besides, the impropriety of obliging such persons to bear arms for the defence of a country, where they look upon themselves as only temporary residents, and liable to be severely punished, should it fall into the hands of their nation, and they were to be found bearing the arms of opposition. And moreover, to force them to learn the use of arms, might be attended with dangerous consequences if they joined with the enemy in time of invasion, or withdrew themselves, as they did before; at any rate they can be of no use whatever in defence of the place.

The subjecting them, therefore, to the payment of a certain yearly sum, instead of obliging them to appear in the field, to which they are so greatly averse, would be the means of a
considerable

considerable saving to Government for arms, powder, and other articles; and some part of it might be applied for furnishing such persons in the militia with regimentals, who can ill afford it themselves. This would be the means of having a complete militia in Dominica, wholly composed of English subjects, on whom alone any dependance can be placed for its defence, should it be invaded, and be so destitute of regular troops, as when it was taken the last war.

CHAPTER XI.

DESCRIPTION OF THE WHITE INHABITANTS, FREE PEOPLE OF COLOUR, AND NATIVE INDIANS OF THE ISLAND; THEIR MANNERS AND CUSTOMS, TOGETHER WITH OBSERVATIONS THEREON.

THE white inhabitants of Dominica are composed of English, French, Spaniards, Italians, and Genoese, who are natives of those countries in Europe, or their issue, born in the West Indies; which latter are called Creoles, to distinguish them from Europeans. There are also some few Americans, white people, who are called American refugees, and who retired thither after the establishment of the last peace, and independence of North America.

The British inhabitants consist of English, Scotch, Irish, and the said American refugees,
who

who altogether, including men, women, and children, do not exceed the number of six hundred, exclusive of the regular troops stationed there. This is indeed a very small number of English subjects for so very large and fine an island, the value of its possession by Great Britain being thereby considerably lessened; for so few inhabitants are totally insufficient to render it of that importance, which it is capable of being, to the mother-country.

The customs and manners of the English are much the same, as distinguish the different descriptions of the same people in the several parts of Great Britain, from whence they came; and their religious persuasions are also the same.

It is much to be lamented, that in the English West India islands in general, there prevails a great aversion to forming matrimonial connections, as colonization is thereby much

much impeded, and many evils, to the difadvantage of the British empire in that part of the world, are thereby greatly promoted. This averfion is, in a great meafure, to be attributed to the views of the generality of Europeans, who having fubmitted to a voluntary exile, which they fuppofe is to be only for a few years, flatter themfelves they fhall foon return wealthy to their own countries. Buoyed up with thefe notions, they look upon matrimony as a bar to their expectations; and in the mean time, content themfelves with the company of a mulatto or negro miftrefs, who brings them a fpurious race of children, the maintenance of whom, together with the extravagance of their fable mothers, foon diffipates the firft favings of their keeper's hard-earned wealth. When, as often is the cafe, worn out by the climate, or other difafters, they at laft fee their folly, but generally too late to prevent its confequences.

But

But were such adventurers only to consider, how few who go to the West Indies live to acquire affluence, or ever return to their own countries; together with the superior advantage to be derived from the society of a wife and children of their own colour, it is probable, that so many would not decline an eligible situation for prospects that are so uncertain.

That which renders this aversion to matrimony the more remarkable is, that the generality of the English white women in the West Indies are as lovely as in any part of the world besides, make as goods wives, tender mothers, and as agreeable companions. It is true, they are not so remarkable for that pleasing florid complexion, which is peculiar to the sex in England; but they have in common as clear white skins, are as delicately and well featured women as in any part of the creation; and they are remarkable for domestic qualifications,

especially

especially for being fine, neat workers at the needle, and making the best nurses, as well as œconomists.

In proof of their conjugal fidelity, such a thing is hardly to be heard of as a Creole woman undergoing that ignominious trial for crim. con. so frequent in the more polite countries of Europe, where also it is too common for the women to form connections with negro men. This last is a thing so very odious in the opinion of Creole white women in general, that the most profligate of them would shudder at the bare idea of submitting to it; and there is hardly to be produced an instance of the kind in the West Indies.

Withal, so very remarkable are the English Creole women for sobriety and chastity, that in the first instance very few of them drink any thing but water, or beverage of lime juice, water, and syrup; and in the latter, that
there

there are few of them to be seen among the loose wantons of the sex in the West Indies; the generality of the white women of that description being actually composed of adventurers from Europe, or of such as have followed the army and navy to the islands.

This last circumstance is, in my opinion, a clear refutation of that too generally received notion, that women in particular, in warm climates, are given to inordinate desires; and proves to a demonstration, that such passions are not owing to the climate, but rather to a too warm constitution, which, aided by luxury, too often gives itself up to satisfying its own depraved appetites, against every sense of decency, and consideration of duty.

These observations lead me to the discussion of another subject, of equal importance; namely, that of education peculiar to the English West India islands. This, although it is a task which I am by no means competent to, yet I shall be happy, if the few observations here offered are of the least use to the rising generation in that part of the British dominions.

It must be confessed, that in the English West Indies education is, in general, too little attended to, owing, in a great measure, to the prejudices of the generality of parents, who, coming themselves from Europe, fancy there is no possibility of getting a good education in any other part of the world.

Prepossessed with this notion, their whole endeavours are to accomplish it for the benefit of their children; who, in the mean time, are usually put under the care of some old woman, or person of the other sex, equally as unqualified to teach them, merely for the purpose of keeping the children out of the way. But it is often the case, that after several years have been spent by a child under such tutors,
some

some unexpected misfortune happens to the parent, who is rendered as unable to afford the expence of sending his children to Europe, and paying the necessary contingencies of schooling there, as he was when they first came into the world; or too much time is required to enable him to accomplish his purpose.

The consequences are obvious, for the child having outgrown the proper season for receiving any material benefit from education, it answers very little purpose, if at that time the parent is able to accomplish his desire. And it is a general remark in the West Indies, that of such as have been sent to Europe for education after a certain period, few have returned thither as accomplished as many, who have had only a moderate schooling in the islands; and scarcely any, without having his morals corrupted.

To this so prevalent practice in parents, of sending their children to Europe for education, it is owing, that there are so very few good school-masters, or other proper persons, to form the minds of youth in the English islands; as the encouragement for such is so very trifling, that it is seldom worth a man's while to attempt it. Whereas, was the contrary practice more in use, there is no doubt but that education would be as attainable in the West Indies, as in any part of Europe, and at a much less expence.

The French inhabitants of Dominica are more numerous than the English; and as before observed, have the most valuable coffee plantations in that island. Their manners and customs differ but little from the people in the other French islands; and their religion is the same, for they are all Roman Catholics.

They have several chapels in the island, but the principal one is in the town of Roseau. This is built of wood, and is neatly ornamented in the inside with an altar-piece, hangings, paintings,

ings, and images of the Virgin Mary and other saints, baptismal font, and pews. Here their bells are continually tinkling for prayers, especially on Sundays and holidays, which last are so very numerous, that they generally occur three or four times every week; when great numbers of the French, both white and coloured people, regularly attend their priests.

The revenues of this chapel, and of the ministers thereof, principally arise from the rents of a large lot of land on which it is built; and which was granted by the English Commissioners, in 1763, to the French inhabitants for that purpose, on lease for ninety-nine years. Great part of this land is let out for the remainder of the term yet to expire; and thereon are built several good houses, the owners of which pay a yearly assessed part of the rent of the same, exclusive of the first cost of the lease of each lot on which the houses are built.

The

The French priests in Dominica are appointed by superiors in the island of Martinique; to the government of which island, and to the laws of their own nation, they consider themselves to be responsible.

The Spanish inhabitants of this island are not very numerous, being only composed of renegados from their own settlements, and are no great credit to this; but are suffered to remain there, by frequently taking the oaths of allegiance to his Britannic Majesty, on their paying a certain sum each time. This they sadly complain of; but they do not mind the oath, as was evident on the day of attack by the French; for on that day several of them joined their countrymen arrived from Martinique, and with large knives and pistols stuck in their belts, were ready to assist to plunder and murder the English inhabitants, had the invasion been made in the night.

The

The Italians and Genoese are also but few, and are chiefly employed in cutting down the trees on the plantations that are in woods: some of them carry about the country articles of grocery, tobacco, and other matters, which they dispose of principally to negros on estates; by which means they make a good livelihood.

The other free inhabitants of this island are free mestiffs, free mulattos, free negros, and native Indians.

The free people of colour are chiefly of French extraction, and most of them came from the islands of that nation; from whence they have retired on account of the severity of the French laws, which prohibit them from wearing shoes, stockings, ornaments, or any dress after the fashion of white people.

They

They are, in general, very idle and insolent; the females usually follow the occupations of pastry-cooks and hucksters, to the great detriment of more industrious poor white people, and will often get credit for articles in their way of business when the latter cannot; but being in general young persons of the sex, they contrive to pay their debts very satisfactorily to some merchants. There are, however, some few of them who are natives of the island, who have good coffee plantations, and are very civil and courteous.

The free people of colour are remarkably fond of dress and dancing; for the enjoyment of both which they will sacrifice every thing that is valuable in their possession. Dancing is the chief part of their amusements, their preparations for which are commonly very expensive; their ladies being usually dressed in silks, silk stockings and shoes; buckles, bracelets, and rings of gold and silver, to a considerable value. Their entertaiments, on these occasions, are also very expensive, their guests being treated with every thing of the best. These meetings sometimes last for two or three days together, during which they dance the whole time almost; but it seldom happens that their balls conclude without broken heads, bloody noses, or some piece of perfect gallantry.

The Indians, natives of Dominica, are descended from the ancient inhabitants, who were found there when this island was first discovered by Europeans, and are the people properly called " Caribbes." Of these there are not more than twenty or thirty families, who have their dwellings on the east part of the island, at a great distance from Roseau, where they are seldom seen.

They are of a clear copper colour, have long, sleek, black hair on their heads; their persons are short, stout, and well made; but they disfigure their faces by pressing flat their noses, which is done in their infancy. They are a very quiet, inoffensive people, speak a language of their own, and French, but none of them speak English.

They live chiefly by fishing in the rivers and the sea, or by fowling in the woods, at both of which they are very expert with their bows and arrows. They will kill the smallest bird with an arrow, or transfix a fish at a great depth in the sea; and are very serviceable to the planters near their settlement, whom they chiefly supply with fish and game. They are also very ingenious, making curious wrought panniers, or baskets of silk grass, or the bark of trees.

It is much to be regretted, that since this island has been in the possession of the English, so little pains have been taken to cultivate an union with these people, as they might be capable of essential service to its internal security, especially against the accumulation of runaway negros in the time of peace; and in war they might be induced to join in its defence, should it be invaded. Yet they are permitted to roam wherever their fancies lead them, as much unnoticed as if no such people were in existence. They are men as well as we, are born with the same degree of sensibility; and by proper encouragement, might be of material benefit to a country which was originally their own.

CHAPTER XII.

OF THE NEGRO SLAVES OF THIS ISLAND, THEIR RE-
BELLION AND REDUCTION THERE; TOGETHER
WITH THE USAGE, MANNERS, CUSTOMS, AND CHA-
RACTERS OF THOSE PEOPLE IN GENERAL IN THE
WEST INDIES.

THE negros in Dominica, under the description of slaves, are between fifteen and sixteen thousand; but not more than one half of that number belongs to the English inhabitants, whose plantations in particular are but thinly furnished with them. This is owing to a variety of causes; and among others, to the rather imprudent conduct of some of the first English settlers, after the country was ceded to Great Britain.

Many of them brought negros who had only been in the capacity of domestics; some, those that were banished from other islands for their

their crimes, and others purchased negros just brought from Africa, for the purpose of settling their new estates. These were immediately set to work, to cut down massy, hard wood trees, to lop and burn the branches, clear the ground of the roots, and to labour at difficult, though necessary business, for which they were by no means qualified.

The consequences of these great mistakes soon after appeared, for the domestic and new negros labouring in such work as they were not used to, in a climate, which, from the abundance of its woods, was so unsettled, that it rained greatest part of the year; whilst they had only temporary huts covered with the branches and leaves of trees to shelter them in at night, and were subject to many inconveniences in the day-time; this very uncomfortable situation occasioned the death of numbers, and caused others to run away into the woods, where many of them perished.

The increase of runaway negros also owes its origin, in a great measure, to the impolitic conduct of some of the first English settlers: for, during the neutral state of this island, a number of French and Spaniards had settled themselves on the most fertile parts of the sea-coasts, and had raised to themselves very fine sugar and coffee estates. Among these were some Jesuits, who having sugar plantations on the south-east part of the island, they disposed of the same, together with the negros on them, to some of the English new settlers.

Many of the negros so purchased from the Jesuits, either from their attachment to them, or dislike to their new masters, soon after betook themselves to the woods with their wives and children, where they were joined, from time to time, by others from different estates. There they secreted themselves for a number

number of years, formed companies under different chiefs, built good houses, and planted gardens in the woods, where they raised poultry, hogs, and other small stock, which, with what the sea, rivers, and woods afforded, and what they got from the negros they had intercourse with on the plantations, they lived very comfortably, and were seldom disturbed in their haunts.

They were not, however, often guilty of any material mischief, and had never committed murder till the reduction of the island by the French; but soon after that happened, the depredations of the runaways began to be of a more serious nature; for they robbed, and destroyed the property, and at length killed some of the English inhabitants.

To the commission of these daring outrages, they were greatly encouraged by the Marquis Duchilleau, who, as before mentioned, had actually engaged with them for defending the island; for which purpose he gave them the muskets and bayonets which he took from the English inhabitants, with powder and balls; and also furnished them with the same provisions as was allowed to the French soldiers.

The runaways, at first, only robbed the English plantations of ground provisions, plantains, bananas, and small stock; but at last they had the audacity to kill and carry away the cattle, and to plunder and set fire to the buildings on the estates.

The first instance of their committing murder happened on a plantation, where a Mr. Hugh Gould was the manager; and who, on their coming there to rob, as they had done several times before, thought proper to oppose them, and actually drove them away. Exasperated at this opposition, they a few days after returned in great numbers, with a determination

mination to kill him; but he, fortunately for him, being gone from the estate on business, escaped their vengeance. However, their bloody intentions were not to be disappointed, and though missing their object, they were resolved to give a sample of their formidable power, and they actually murdered a Mr. Grahame, who resided with the manager as a companion. Him they shot on his knees, as he was begging for mercy, using him in the most shocking, barbarous manner while he was dying; and after stripping the house of every thing of value, they set it on fire.

Alarmed at this daring wickedness of the runaway negros, the English inhabitants on the neighbouring estates, apprehensive of their own danger, applied to the Marquis Duchilleau for protection, to grant them arms, with liberty to defend themselves, and to apprehend the runaways who had murdered a white man. These requests were, however, refused by that Governor,

Governor, and he actually threatened, that if they dared to attempt any thing against those people he would imprison them, or send them off the island; at the same time, he acknowledged that the runaways were his friends.

They, encouraged by this uncommon conduct of this French Governor, were afterwards fearless of any mischief they did, coming in large bodies, all armed with muskets, bayonets, and cutlasses, on what plantations they thought proper to rob, in the open day. Nay, they often came in the same manner, with conk shells blowing and French colours flying, close to the town of Roseau in the day-time, and in sight of the French soldiers.

Driven to the greatest distress, and in dread of being destroyed by those cruel wretches, the English planters, on the interior plantations, were constrained to abandon their estates,

and

and to retire with their families to Roseau, as the only means of saving their lives, leaving their property to the mercy of the runaways.

After they had done considerable mischief, but were still pursuing their destructive operations against the English inhabitants, unnoticed by the Marquis Duchilleau, it was found necessary to petition the Marquis de Bouillé at Martinico, setting forth the distressed situation of the English planters in this island; praying for arms, with permission to defend themselves against the runaway negros, and to endeavour to apprehend such of them as had been guilty of murder.

In consequence of this petition, the Marquis de Bouillé gave directions to the Governor of Dominica, to give arms to such of the English as were on the plantations, to endeavour to put a stop to the sanguinary and shocking ravages committed against them, and to send out parties in the woods to apprehend the runaways, in order to their being punished for such daring crimes.

These orders of the Marquis were accordingly put into execution; and though attended with no material service, in point of reducing the runaways, yet were the means of preventing, in a great measure, their further depredations, till after the island was restored to the English. However, at times, they still robbed the estates of provisions; especially plantations that were nigh their camps in the woods, yet not in so daring a manner as they had done heretofore, doing it generally in the most secret manner, in the night-time, when they were under no dread of being apprehended.

This dread was, however, not occasioned by any apprehensions of being opposed by the English inhabitants, as afterwards appeared;
but

but from that of the parties, who used at times to be sent out after them in the woods. But these latter being composed only of people of colour, were no ways industrious in that service, and actually never apprehended one of them. In this respect, however, an English manager of a plantation, Mr. John Tombs, had much greater success; for on the runaways coming to rob the estate on which he lived, he opposed them, and actually took some of them prisoners.

But being apprehensive, that those who escaped being taken might, with others, take an opportunity to revenge the loss of their companions and booty, he contrived to learn their intentions, by means of a trusty negro belonging to the estate, whom he sent into the woods, as if he were a runaway himself, on account of bad usage.

Mr. Tombs having procured several blunderbusses and muskets for the occasion, instructed

structed the other negro men of the plantation in their use; exercising them for several days previous to the intended attack, which he was informed, by his faithful spy, was to be made on such a day, in the night-time, when the runaways thought to take him in bed, and intended putting him to death in a most cruel manner.

They accordingly made their attempt on the very day he was advised of, coming in great numbers, about midnight, to the estate, with expectations of glutting their vengeance. Fearful of giving the alarm, or making their approach known, as soon as they came out of the woods, near the borders of the estate, they extinguished their lighted flambeaux, marching silently along in the road that lead to the manager's house, wholly unapprehensive of danger.

As soon as they had put out their lights, their guide, the faithful spy, left them, and joined his master, acquainting him of their approach, and, with those that were with him, immediately on hearing the trampling of the feet of the runaways, fired a smart volley from their blunderbusses and muskets among them.

This unexpected discharge, so seasonably made, put the assailants into great confusion; from which however recovering, they returned the fire for some time, but so uncertain and irregular, that it did no execution. This was, however, not the case from the fire of Mr. Tombs and his party, as was evident from the cries and groans heard among the runaways, who were at last obliged to betake themselves to flight; yet they took their killed and wounded into the woods with them.

It is remarkable, that on this occasion neither Mr. Tombs, nor any of his people were hurt

hurt by the fire from the runaways, although this conflict with them lasted near half an hour. Whilst, on the other side, there could be no doubt but that they suffered considerably, both in killed and wounded, from the great quantity of blood seen on the spot, and traced to the woods, the next morning; but the number of either was never afterwards known, the runaways having adopted the policy of the French in that respect.

This action was greatly to the credit of Mr. Tombs, and was of eminent service at that time to the English planters of the island; as the runaways finding how much it was in the power of a single white man of resolution to oppose them, afterwards kept themselves pretty peaceable, till the French quitted possession of the country. But shortly after that happened they re-commenced their depredations, notwithstanding several proclamations were issued by the Legislature of the island,

offering

offering a pardon to all that would surrender themselves, except such as had been guilty of murder.

To these proclamations the runaways paid no manner of attention; but on the contrary, they bid defiance to every measure, and had the audacity to threaten, they would repel any attempts to be made to reduce them. In consequence of this obstinacy of theirs, and their still continued acts of mischief on the plantations, an act of the colony was passed for raising a fund, to be applied to the purpose of forcing them into subjection. This act was made to be in force for three years, commencing in 1785, and was made by way of tax in the following manner, that is to say,

£.	s.	d.	
10	0	0	Per cent. on the assessed value of rent on all houses in the towns.
5	0	0	Per cent. on the assessed value of rent on all vacant lots.
16	10	0	Per

£. s. d.

16 10 0 Per annum to be paid by all practitioners of physic in the island.

16 10 0 Per annum to be paid by all practitioners of the law.

13 4 0 Per annum to be paid by each merchant.

13 4 0 Per annum to be paid by each vendue master, tavern-keeper, &c.

13 4 0 Per annum to be paid by each merchant or shop-keeper (aliens.)

3 6 0 Per annum to be paid by each manager and overseer of plantations in the island, whose salary was 200l. per annum.

1 13 0 Per annum to be paid by each manager and overseer, whose salary was 100l. per annum.

1 13 0 Per annum to be paid by every other white man in the island.

1 13 0 Per annum to be paid by each male person of colour.

2 10 0 Per

£.	s.	d.	
2	10	0	Per cent. on all merchandize.
2	10	0	Per cent. on all goods sold at vendue.
1	0	0	Per annum for every negro slave, tradesman, or porter.
0	10	0	Per annum for every house negro and slave on the plantations.
0	10	0	Per annum for every hogshead of sugar made in the island.
0	6	0	Per annum for every tierce of sugar.
0	3	0	Per annum for every barrel of sugar.
0	8	3	Per annum for every hogshead of coffee.
0	5	0	Per annum for every tierce of coffee.
0	3	0	Per annum for every barrel of coffee.
0	1	0	Per annum for every 100lb. of coffee in bags.
0	6	0	Per annum for every hogshead of rum.
0	4	6	Per annum for every tierce of rum.
0	3	0	Per annum for every barrel of rum.

The

The next step taken by the Legislature for reducing the runaways to obedience was, to raise a body of colony legions, composed of white men, free people of colour, and able negro men belonging to the different plantations, for the purpose of sending them after the runaways into the woods. Three separate encampments, formed by these legions, were established near the haunts of the runaways, against whom operations were immediately commenced; but it was a long time before any material service could be effected against them; they, in the mean while, committing the most shocking ravages, almost within sight of their opponents.

The number of the legions was about five hundred men, under the command of able officers of the regiment then stationed there; and who, with a number of privates of the same regiment, became volunteers in the service,

the most daring outrages on the plantations.—
The number of persons, of which the legion
was composed, was about five hundred, under the command of officers of the 30th regiment of foot, at that time stationed in the
island; these officers, with several soldiers of
the same regiment, became volunteers in that
service, and had extra pay from the colony;
the pay of each person employed on the occasion being as follows:

	£.	s.	d.	
Captain	1	13	0	
Lieutenant	1	4	9	
Serjeant	0	12	0	
Corporal	0	9	0	per day.
Private	0	8	3	
Surgeon	0	16	6	
Carriers	0	3	0	

The runaways fully acquainted with the
measures taken against them, yet confiding in

the strength of their numbers, and the difficult access to their camps in the woods, made no offer to surrender themselves; but rather seemed determined to abide by the consequences, and deriding the attempt of reducing them by force, threatened to do still greater mischiefs. They accordingly did as they had threatened, beginning their attack on the plantation of Thomas Osborn, Esq. coming there in the night, and doing considerable damage; in drawing off some rum by the light of their torches, it caught fire, which being communicated to the buildings on the estate, burnt them down to the ground.

Their next attack was soon after on a sugar plantation at Rosalie, belonging to the Lieutenant-governor and other persons in England. There they came also in the night-time, murdered Mr. Gamble, the manager, Mr. Armstrong, carpenter, Mr. Hatton, and Mr. Lile, the overseers, together with the chief negro driver

driver belonging to the estate. Having glutted themselves with murdering these persons, after stripping them of their cloaths, they set fire round the bodies; doing the same to the sugar works, principal buildings, and canes; and committing other confiderable damages, to the amount of several thousand pounds.

Elated with their success, and having satiated themselves for that time with murder, plunder, and devastation, they retired to the dwelling-house on the estate, where they regaled on the stock, provisions, and liquors they found in plenty, their chiefs being served in the filver veffels of the Lieutenant-governor, which, together with other valuable articles, to a great amount, they afterwards carried away with them. On this plantation they continued two days, riotting and revelling, blowing conk fhells and huzzaing, as for a great victory, having taken the precaution to stop up the roads to the estate by felling large trees, and placing centinels to give them notice, in case of the approach of the legions.

The latter were, at the same time, in their encampments in the woods, while the runaways were committing these horrid transactions, the knowledge of which was first brought to Roseau, where it produced the greatest consternation, as it did also throughout the island. This matter occasioned the legions to be greatly blamed for their want of attention to their duty; as there was every reason to suppose, that had they been more diligent in their search after the runaways, they would never have dared to commit such wanton mischiefs, or might have been apprehended in the act. It was not, however, so much the fault of the legions, as it was of the chief managers of the business; who being but little acquainted with the situation of the woods, had so disposed the stations of the three encampments, that they were unable to do any effectual

tual service; and it is probable, that the runaways would never have been reduced, in the manner they were soon after, had it not been for the exertions of some private persons, who materially promoted it.

Of these, a Mr. John Richardson deserves to be noticed, as having several times offered his services for the purpose, which had been rejected; yet, grieving to see the business so very ill managed, he formed a plan, to shew how easy it was to reduce the runaways, by boldly attacking them in their camps.

As he was a carpenter, he was employed to rebuild the works lately destroyed by the runaways on the Rosalie estate; and being at work there, it happened that a party of the legions called there in the way to their camp, in order to refresh themselves. Mr. Richardson prevailed on them to accompany him, for the purpose of attacking a principal runaway chief, whose name was "Balla," who was the commander of their late expedition against that estate; and whose haunt Mr. Richardson very well knew, having a long while before attacked him there.

Mr. Richardson having strengthened this party, with the addition of some trusty negro men of the estate, they set out one evening on their expedition, and having travelled all night through the woods, wading through rapid rivers, crossing over steep mountains, and encountering many difficulties in their way, by noon the next day they came to the mountain whereon was the encampment of Balla. This they ascended with great difficulty, it being cut into steps of a great height above each other, which had been done by the runaways for their own convenience, as being the only possible way to ascend the mountain.

These steps the party were obliged to go up, one after the other, and to have their muskets
handed

handed to them, the one on the upper, by him on the step below, till they were all ascended. Mr. Richardson was the first on the landing-place on the top of the mountain, where hiding himself among some bushes, he perceived the runaways going in and out of their houses, preparing their dinners, little expecting such troublesome guests. As soon as the whole of the party had joined him, they rushed on towards the houses, shouting and keeping up a brisk firing from their muskets on the runaways; who, in the greatest dismay and confusion, betook themselves to flight, throwing themselves down the steep sides of the mountain, in their hurry to get out of the way, by which it is probable that several of them were killed.

The party having thus taken possession of the runaways camp, immediately began to destroy it, by setting fire to the houses; but in searching them previous thereto, they found some women and children, among whom was a son of Balla's, who, with the rest, they took prisoners. Whilst searching the houses, the runaways on the opposite mountain, on which they had retired, having recovered a little from their fright, and probably discerning the small number of the party, made several attempts to return and recover their camp, keeping up a smart firing for some time, from the place they were on. But they were discouraged by a well-timed thought of Mr. Richardson's, who, as often as they seemed determined to return, called out the names of the different commanding officers of the legions to attack the runaways, " To the right or left," according to the side on which they kept firing from the opposite mountain. This had the desired effect, making them believe they were surrounded by the legions; the apprehensions of which caused the runaways to abandon the place with the same precipitation they had quitted their camp, leaving it in peaceable possession of the party.

The

The latter then had leisure to do their business, and to examine the rest of the houses, which they found well furnished with provisions, a vast quantities of cloaths, valuable articles of furniture, and several other things, which they had stolen from the different plantations. Such articles of value as they could carry the party took with them, after destroying such as the fire could not injure, and burning the houses, they descended with their prisoners, and returned home in safety, none of the party being hurt on the occasion.

This was a capital check to the runaways, and reflects great honour on Mr. Richardson; as by his means it was, in a great measure, that the runaways were at that time reduced. For after this action they dispersed, and were so much disheartened, that they never afterwards dared to assemble in any great numbers together; but flying from place to place in the woods, were either killed, taken, or surrendered themselves; and this noted chief, Balla, soon after fell into the

the hands of a party of the legions, by whom he was killed.

The runaway negros have since then, been seldom heard of in Dominica; for those that were there under another chief, named Farcel*, it is imagined have quitted the island, and have retired among the French settlements, or among the Carribbees at Saint Vincent's.

It is computed, that the number of them that were killed, taken, or that surrendered, during this contest, was about one hundred and fifty. The expences of the colony, on this occasion, was upwards of fifty

* Since this work has been sent to the press, advice has been received from Dominica, that the runaways, under the command of this chief, having been joined by a number of other negro slaves, from different plantations of the French inhabitants, have again commenced depredations of a most serious nature in that island. To this the report further mentions, they have been encouraged by the disturbances which at present prevail in the island of Martinique, occasioned by the late revolution in France. But the particulars of this new rebellion of the negros in Dominica have not yet come to the knowledge of the Author, with sufficient authenticity for insertion.

thousand pounds current money of the island; a sum so considerable, that it appears hardly credible how, or in what manner it was raised and applied. The first I have endeavoured to give some idea of in the former part of this chapter; and for the satisfaction of the reader, shall here give a statement of the first year's amount of the taxes, which were raised for this particular purpose; that is to say, from the 1st of May, 1785, to the 1st of May, 1786, as follows:

	£.	s.	d.
Amount of tax on 4702 hogsheads of sugar, at 10s. each	2351	0	0
Ditto on 571 tierces of ditto, at 6s. each	171	6	0
Ditto on 745 barrels of ditto, at 3s. each	111	15	0
Ditto on 1861 hogsheads of coffee, at 8s. 3d. each	767	13	3
Ditto on 122 tierces of ditto, at 5s. each	30	10	0

Amount

	£.	s.	d.
Amount of tax on 503 barrels of coffee, at 3s. each	75	9	0
Ditto on 84340 lb. in bags of ditto, at 1s. per cwt.	42	3	4
Ditto on 682 hogsheads of rum at 6s. each	204	12	0
Ditto on 73 tierces of ditto, at 4s. 6d. each	16	8	6
Ditto on 109 casks of ditto, at 3s. each	16	7	0
Ditto on merchants and traders	676	10	0
Ditto on managers and overseers	122	2	0
Ditto on Aliens	726	0	0
Ditto on inhabitants (poll tax)	1206	6	0
Ditto on 597 negro slaves (tradesmen)	597	0	0
Ditto on 12429 ditto, domestics and field negros	6214	10	0
Ditto on rents of houses and lots in the towns	1397	10	0
Ditto on taverns, &c.	1256	10	0

Amount

	£.	s.	d.
Amount of tax on manumitting slaves	198	0	0
Fines of the militia	29	14	0
Arrears of taxes	803	1	9½
Total	17014	7	10½

This tax, as before observed, was made to be in force for three years; and although it has, in some measure, answered the end for which it was imposed, has been a very heavy burden on the colony, and might, had the business it was intended for been properly managed, have been lessened to within little more than the first year's amount.

The negro slaves in Dominica are, in general, comfortably situated, and well treated, especially on the plantations; where, if they are industrious, they have the means of living in a manner very different from that deplorable

state,

state, which some people in England have been at the pains to represent, as the case in general of slaves in the British islands. They have there as much land as they chuse to cultivate for their own use, are capable of raising great quantities of all manner of ground provisions, garden stuff, and other things, with which they actually supply the markets every Sunday, and some of them to a considerable amount.

They likewise breed hogs, rabbits, fowls, and other small stock for themselves; and many of them, who are careful in raising such provisions, acquire a very comfortable living, exclusive of what is allowed them by their owners. They have, moreover, many opportunities on the plantations to procure other things to sell, or make use of themselves, which are not to be had in many other islands, as plenty of fish in the rivers, crapaux, wild yams, and other articles in the woods; by which,

those

those who are industrious in their leisure hours often make tolerable sums of money.

However, not intending to confine myself to observations on the treatment of negro slaves of this island in particular, in order to avoid being singular in that respect, I shall extend my remarks on that subject to the usage, manners, and customs relative to them in the English West Indies in general.

The slaves then, in all the British West India settlements, are by no means treated in that harsh, cruel, and barbarous manner, which some have described, to impress the minds, and to impose on the judgment of this nation. For, on the contrary, the treatment they receive from their owners, is, as nearly as can be, that of a parent to his children.

Every

Every family has a good comfortable house to reside in, which is built at the expence of their masters; who also furnish them with such cloaths as is necessary for them, with a doctor, medicines, and all things needful when sick; and have nothing to expect from them in return but good behaviour, and a necessary degree of labour for the service of his plantation.

He moreover gives them a weekly allowance of provisions, consisting of biscuit, Indian corn, beans, salt fish, mackrel, or herrings; which, together with what they are able, if industrious, to supply themselves with from their own gardens, and the produce of their own stock, they are enabled to live in a manner which is by no means unenviable, and preferable to the situation of thousands of people in Great Britain, with all the accompaniments of their fancied liberties.

The

The labour of the negros on the plantations is by no means burdenfome, or difficult; the digging cane holes, and cutting down canes, being the chief part of their bufinefs, at either of which a labouring white man, even there, will do nearly double the work of a negro in a day. Exclufive of thefe, the labour of the flaves is moftly confined to carrying dung in fmall bafkets, planting, and weeding the canes. The making fugar, rum, and other articles, is the employment of fuch negros only, as have been taught thofe bufineffes; and for which they have good encouragement to be induftrious, by extra provifions, cloaths, and other things, given them while employed.

The field negros, when digging cane holes, have ufually, in the afternoon, half a pint of rum and water, fweetened with molaffes, given to each of them, which is a great refrefhment in that labour, and caufes them to work with

chear-

chearfulneſs. It is pleaſing to ſee them at this work, they being all together in one row, like a regiment of ſoldiers, and all their hoes moving together; the women ſinging ſome ludicrous ſongs of their own compoſing, which are anſwered in the ſame manner by the men, and each ſtriving to outdo the other. This has a good effect in ſoftening their labour, and is much promoted by giving them their rum and water, which they have alſo ſometimes in their other work, eſpecially after having been in the rain.

The proportion of the working field negros on each plantation is, commonly, from one third to two fifths of the whole number belonging to each eſtate; the remainder include tradeſmen, watchmen, ſtock-keepers, invalids, houſe-ſervants, nurſes, and young children.

They have generally one day in every week, out of crop time, or the Saturday afternoon allowed

allowed them, for the purpose of working their own gardens, exclusive of their leisure hours, which are from twelve till two o'clock in the afternoon of every day, and Sundays. But was the custom to be general, of allowing them one day in every week out of crop time, the necessity for their working their gardens on Sundays might be prevented, and that day wholly appropriated by them to religious duties, which might probably be the means of promoting good order amongst those people, and securing their future welfare.

The French planters in all the settlements belonging to that nation have their negros baptized, and taught some prayers, which they repeat on their knees every morning before they go to work, and every evening after finishing it. This has a good effect on their conduct, attaches them to the interests of their masters, cements their union with each other, and is productive of many advantages to the French planters,

planters, who, notwithstanding their being actually more rigid to their negros than the English, yet have better and more faithful slaves.

Once a year, the following articles of cloathing are distributed among the slaves on every English plantation, viz. a good warm jacket, frock, trowsers, and hat for each man and boy; a jacket, wrapper, petticoat, and hat for each woman and girl. These are furnished them at the expence of their masters, and are generally given to them at Christmas; at which time they are allowed three days holidays, viz. Christmas day and two days after; during which time they do no work, but spend it in dancing, singing, and making merry.

This they are enabled to do, by having also given them at this time four or five pounds of meat, the same quantity of flour or rice, with some rum and sugar to each negro, besides taking from their own stock, kids, pigs, or fowls; with which they feast one another during the holidays. At this time especially, they dress themselves out in their best cloaths; many of them in good linen, silk handkerchiefs, bracelets and ear-rings of gold and silver, to no inconsiderable amount, in which they visit or receive their acquaintances from the neighbouring estates.

At this time too, they perform their offerings of victuals on the graves of their deceased relations and friends; a piece of superstition which all negros are addicted to, and which, were they to neglect doing, they firmly believe they would be punished by the spirits of the deceased persons. This offering consists of meat, whole kids, pigs, or fowls, with broth, liquors, and other matters; and is performed in the following manner: a man or woman accuſtomed to the ceremony, takes of each meat laid in diſhes round the grave, and pulling ſome of it in pieces, throws the ſame on the grave, calling out the name of the dead perſon as if alive, ſaying, "Here is a "piece of ſuch a thing for you to eat; why "did you leave your father, mother, wife, "children and friends? Did you go away "angry with us? When ſhall we ſee you "again? Make our proviſions to grow, and "ſtock to breed; don't let any body do us "harm, and we will give you the ſame next "year;" with the like expreſſions to every thing they throw on the grave. After which, taking a little of the rum or other liquors, they ſprinkle it thereon, crying out in the ſame manner, "Here is a little rum to "comfort your heart, good bye to you, "God bleſs you;" and drinking ſome of it themſelves to the welfare of the deceaſed, they ſet up a diſmal cry and howling, but immediately after begin to dance and ſing

round

round the grave. The ceremony is then concluded, by every one scrambling for the remainder of the offering left in the dishes, the dogs devouring that on the grave; and the company bidding their dead friends adieu for that time, they all depart to their houses, and continue their merriment the whole day after. This practice is truly laughable to white people who see it; but it is a plain indication, that negros have some notion of the immortality of the soul.

The slaves belonging to people in the towns of the English islands, are composed of house servants, tradesmen and porters. The first live much in the same manner as the common servants in England, but do not half as much work, and are subject only to a moderate manual correction, instead of being discharged for their faults, and left a burden on the public; or to support themselves, driven to the necessity of using such means, as to forfeit their lives to the laws; the case too often of servants in England.

The domestic negros are fed, cloathed, and provided with every necessary by their owners, have generally a good apartment in the yard of their masters, to retire and to sleep in; and they are in general well treated. They make tolerable good cooks, washers, and attendants; but it is best not to trust them without check, as stewards, butlers, or in the like offices. They will seldom do the duty, or assist one another in their several departments, without being obliged to it by their masters, whom, however, they seldom scruple to disobey.

The negro slaves, tradesmen, are chiefly carpenters, coopers, blacksmiths, or masons; some of whom make tolerably good workmen, if under proper directions; but they are not very skilful in laying out work themselves, or contriving. They in general live very comfortable,

fortable, are well treated, and many of them make tolerable sums of money by jobs they do for others in their own leisure hours.

The negro porters are in general a very idle, insolent and thievish set of people, and are often guilty of much imposition, especially to strangers on their arrival in the islands. They are commonly the stoutest and worst disposed negros belonging to white people, or to free people of colour in the towns, and pay their owners a certain sum daily; but many of them will game away the whole of their earnings, or spend it in liquor, to the great injury of their masters.

The characters of negros are not so various as one would imagine they would be, from the difference of the country they are brought from, to the West Indies; as very few of them on their arrival in the islands have the least appearance of having been civilized, or possessed of any endowments but such as are merely natural.

For

For the generality of them, on their first introduction, appear as wild as the brute beasts; are indolent and stupid to a degree, so that they hardly know the use of the most common utensil of husbandry, much less the methods of cultivating the ground.

Every thing appears to them as entirely new, as to the infant just come to a moderate degree of vision; but, at the same time, they seem to be so very unconcerned at the sight of the most novel objects, that the bare recollection is not a moment in their minds. They appear insensible to every thing but hunger and thirst, which however, to satisfy, they have no more nicety than a hog; as any thing, either raw or dressed, is equally acceptable when given to them.

This stupidity of theirs continues a length of time after their arrival in the islands, before most of them can be brought to any degree of proper comprehenfion; and with many of them, it is entirely unconquerable.

The Creole negros, that is to fay, thofe who are born in the Weft Indies, having been brought up among white people, and paid fome attention to from their infancy, lofe much of that uncommon ftupidity fo confpicuous in their new negro parents; and are in general tolerably fenfible, fharp, and fagacious. But there is actually fomething fo very unaccountable in the genius of all negros, fo very different from that of white people in general, that there is not to be produced an inftance in the Weft Indies, of any of them ever arriving to any degree of perfection in the liberal arts or fciences, notwithftanding the greateft pains taken with them; and the only thing they are remarkable for attaining to any degree of perfection, is Mufick.

Negros are in general much addicted to witchcraft and idolatry, both of which seem to be inherent in them, so that though many of them profess the Christian Religion, especially that of the Roman Catholicks, and some of them pay great attention thereto, yet, in all matters which concern themselves, they have recourse to their superstitious confidence in the power of the dead, of the sun and moon; nay, even of sticks, stones, and earth from graves hung in bottles in their gardens.

Their superstitious notions with respect to their dead are truly ridiculous, for they suppose that the deceased both eat and drink in their coffins; and for that purpose, they put therein articles for both, together with a pipe and tobacco, and such things as they know the deceased was fond of in his life time. Moreover, at their funerals they believe the dead body has the power of compelling

pelling them to carry it to the grave, in which road it likes, to shew its resentment to those who have offended it; by the coffin's tumbling off the shoulders of the bearer, making them stand stock still, or running therewith with speed, now one way, then another, and sometimes throwing down and trampling on the people who stand in the way.

They have their necromancers and conjurors of both sexes, whom they call " Obeah men and women," to whom they apply for spells and charms against sickness, to prevent their being robbed, or to find out the thief, and to punish those who do them any injury. These Obeah people are very artful in their way, and have a great ascendancy over the other negros, whom they persuade that they are able to do many miracles by means of their art; and very often get good sums of money for their imaginary charms.

The

The method of treating such as apply to these conjurors for curing any imaginary disorder, excited by lowness of spirits or fearful dreams, is very laughable; they persuade them that they are possessed by the devil, as a punishment for some hidden crime; but if not well paid for it, besides promising to submit to every direction of the Obeah master, he will not undertake the cure. Every preliminary being settled between the patient and the operator, the latter begins his work with mumbling over a few strange words, and having every thing ready, the patient so placed in a dark room, that he cannot discover the cheat, he pinches and pulls him till the other cries out with the pain; after which, the conjuror produces sticks, knives, pieces of glass, and even whole bottles, which he persuades the other that he actually took out of the place he complained of; and then, rubbing it over with grease and soot, or some such

such thing, the simple patient believes himself to be perfectly cured.

Strange as this circumstance must appear, it is actually no less true; and many instances have been known in the West Indies, of negros who have been persuaded by these Obeah people, that they were possessed in this manner, till they have killed themselves in despair.

These people are very dangerous on any plantations, for although there is no credit to be given to the power of their pretended charms, yet, they are in general well acquainted with the quality of many poisonous herbs that grow in the West Indies, and which they often give to others who apply to them for charms to be administered to the persons upon whom they are to operate. By this means many white people have been killed by poison under the persuasion of these Obeah men,

men, that it was to make them love their flaves by whom it was obtained.

Negros are in general much addicted to drunkennefs, thievery, incontinency, and idlenefs. The firft vice very few of them will refrain from when they can get liquor, and in their fits of this kind, many of them are very mifchievous.

Thieving from their owners they look upon as no crime, nor have they any dread of being punifhed for it, if they do it without detection; and fo general is this crime, that there goes a proverb current in all the iflands, " Shew me a negro, and I will fhew " you a thief," but were their offences of this nature to be as often and as feverely punifhed there as in England, there would feldom pafs a day, without fome example or other.

So

So little are the sexes attached to each other, or constant in connubial connections, that it is common for the men to have several wives at a time, besides transient mistresses; and the women to leave their husbands for others, and to submit to the embraces of white men for money or fine clothes. Mothers will dispose of their virgin daughters to white men for a moderate sum, nor do they look upon it as any crime, but an honour to the damsel, who is thereby better qualified for being afterwards taken to wife by one of her own colour.

Idleness is so very predominant in negros, especially those brought to the island immediately from Africa, and their dislike of labour is so great, that it is very difficult to make them work: it is sometimes absolutely necessary to have recourse to measures that appear cruel, in order to oblige them to labour. Nay, very often the same means must be used to make them work for themselves, to dress their own victuals, or to keep themselves free from vermine. This vice is so very remarkable in many negros, that they will actually very often, under some tree, sleep out the hours allowed them to get their victuals in, rather than be at the pains of going home to dress them. They are obliged to be attended by the overseers and drivers to make them work their own gardens, at times allowed them for that purpose, which many of them would otherwise spend in sleeping, or doing less necessary things for themselves. Many instances have been known of negros who have unfeelingly endured the pains of the jiggers, by suffering them to breed in their flesh, their feet swelled and perforated like an honey-comb, rather than be at the trouble of taking them out*.

There

---

* The jigger is an insect much like a flea, which penetrates into the flesh of people, especially in the feet; there lays its eggs, hatches them, and if permitted by not taking them out in time, will consume the whole foot.

They

There are however many negros, especially among the Creoles, who are very induſtrious, make good huſbands and wives, tender parents, faithful and diligent ſervants, are obliging and kind to their fellow ſervants, and reſpectful to all deſcriptions of white people. Theſe in return receive every advantage ariſing from ſo proper a conduct; are well treated, encouraged, and protected; and though ſlaves, their ſituation is far more deſirable than that of many white people, in the Weſt Indies, or in Europe.

They give great pain, and have been known to cauſe the amputation of the legs of ſeveral, who have been ſo imprudent as to neglect taking them out; and ſome have loſt their lives by the ſame neglect.

CHAPTER XIII.

OF THE PRESENT TRADE OF THE ISLAND, THE FREE PORT OF ROSEAU, WITH REMARKS ON THE SAME, AND THE CONCLUSION OF THE WHOLE.

THE trade of Dominica is at present very much circumscribed, as except that carried on by a few Guinea Factors, and five or six ships annualy to take away the produce, there is very little commerce in the island.

Roseau is however a free port, but its being so at present is rather a disadvantage to the inhabitants, as it is confined to within little more than one half its former boundaries, and is besides under and subject to so severe regulations and restrictions, that foreigners are deterred, rather than encouraged to trade thither; and they absolutely look upon this free port, in its present situation, as only a snare laid to allure them to certain ruin.

No foreign vessel is allowed to enter this port, if it appear to be any thing above the burthen prescribed by the free-port act, which is there too rigidly construed. For, as the West-India vessels are built for sailing fast, in order to make short voyages, they will not stow away goods equal to their measurement, like the vessels built in England. This has, however, been often made a pretence for even seizing vessels, or obliging them to quit the port; notwithstanding their having on board only money to a great amount to purchase negroes with; by which means the Guinea Factors lost those opportunities of disposing of their slaves, and were thereby disabled from making so early or so great remittances to their correspondents in England, as they would otherwise have done, to the great injury of them both.

The frequent seizures that have been made there, and condemning a number of foreign vessels, under the smallest appearance of their using a clandestine trade, have effectually put a stop to the resort of foreigners thither; nor can the Americans, from having been repeatedly refused admittance, be induced to have any manner of dealings with this island.

Many of the seizures made in this port have been perfectly illegal; as in the case of a French vessel named the Pearl, which having only touched at an out bay in distress for water, was seized, brought to Roseau, and there condemned and sold, with a valuable cargo of sugar. This proceeding was however, by an appeal of the owners to the Admiralty Court in England, greatly reprehended; and that Court adjudged the vessel and cargo to be restored, with full costs and damages, to be paid by those who had been guilty of making so very illegal a seizure.

Moreover,

Moreover, no boat from a foreign vessel is permitted to land on any occasion in this port, but only in a particular spot appointed for the purpose, for if an attempt be made to land at any other place, they are immediately fired at by a centinel on the spot. This is a most extraordinary, as well as a dangerous regulation, and has several times been very nigh proving fatal to both foreigners and the inhabitants of the town. As the former, not apprehending any danger from landing in a different place, have been fired at, and the balls dropt into the boat where the latter have been at work.

In short, so many very extraordinary measures are used for regulating the free port of Roseau, that it is of no manner of advantage to the inhabitants of the place; and in consequence by no means answers the ends for which was appointed by the Crown.

This is a matter worthy of serious consideration by the British Government, as from the still unsettled state of this valuable island the only way to render it of that importance to the mother country, of which it is so eminently capable, will be by a proper encouragement to trade; without which, no settlement in the West-Indies, be its internal resources ever so extensive, can possibly be of any material advantage to whatever nation it belongs.

There seems, however, to be a want of knowledge somewhere of the capabilities of this island; otherwise, there is every reason to believe that it would not have been so greatly neglected as it has been since its restoration to the British dominions, when at the same time, the other powers of Europe were using every means to establish their West-India settlements; the Spaniards, especially in their island of Trinidad, inviting foreigners, particularly English subjects, to reside there, by offering them free grants of land and other great privileges; by which means thousands have quitted the British settlements and gone there,

there, and many from Dominica; whereby the English subjects of this island are reduced to near half the number that were in it, shortly after the restoration, and the generality of them there at present seem disposed to quit it, by reason of the ruin of their trade, and other disadvantageous circumstances which they labour under.

Emigrations of English subjects from our other settlements, or even from Great Britain, might be turned to great advantage to the island of Dominica; as the lands there, if cleared of the excessive forests of woods, are capable of far greater improvements than the lands of Trinidad, or of any other still unsettled country in the West-Indies. And if ample encouragement was to be given by Great Britain, there is no doubt, but that in a few years this island would be in a very flourishing situation.

This might be done, by giving free grants of the unappropriated lands in the interior

Northern parts of the island, which are all in standing woods, in allotments of a certain number of acres to every family, to furnish them that were not able to do it themselves, with provisions and utensils for eighteen months by Government, in order to induce them to reside on the lands, to clear and cultivate the same; after which, their own industry might enable them to proceed.

Secondly, to grant the leasehold lands which have been purchased from the French inhabitants by English subjects, in the same manner as their other lands; a considerable part of them so purchased being now under cultivation, as sugar estates.

Thirdly, the remaining instalments due on lands in this island, not under cultivation, to be given up by Government.

Fourthly, that some mode be adopted for getting the abandoned estates re-cultivated.

And

And lastly, the establishing a society for promoting agriculture in this island, with premiums to be given to such as raise the greatest quantities of West-India produce, for the maintenance of themselves and slaves at first, afterwards for commerce.

If pasture estates were to be established there, as in Jamaica, it would be a material point gained. And as the cattle in Dominica breed extremely well, there is no doubt, but that in a few years, by good management, this island would be well furnished with those useful animals.

The very bad state of the public roads is a great disadvantage to the island, as some of them are perfectly dangerous to travel; and the whole of them are difficult and badly situated. They are in general dug on the sides of mountains of stupendous heights above the rivers or sea, the billows of which are continually dashing at the feet of them, in a frightful

ful manner. They are also so very narrow in some places, that it is very difficult, as well as dangerous, for two persons meeting on horseback to pass each other; as the least slip on the edge would precipitate both the horse and rider to inevitable destruction.

Of this description, are several parts of the road from Roseau to Prince Rupert's Bay; where, together with the frightful prospect of hanging rocks and large stones at a great height above one's head, that threaten every moment to fall and crush the fearful traveller; the tedious steepness, stony, and difficult passages, render them perfectly uncomfortable to travellers.

The public roads in the interior parts of the country are no less inconvenient, they being in general very steep of ascent; narrow, and subject to breaking in. One walks or rides there at a height far exceeding that of the monument in London; so that a person's head turns giddy on casting a view to the bottom, as he passes along.

Those who are advocates for the abolition of slavery, may in this island have the opportunity of trying the settlement of cool situations by white people only. Why not employ the soldiers there, and allow them extra pay for making good bridle roads in the interior parts of this country? this would materially promote the further settlement of the island; and was a good open road to be made from Roseau to Prince Rupert's Bay, the communication between those two places would be productive of the greatest utility, as other roads might be made to branch from it to the windward and leward coasts, in a much more convenient manner than can be done by the present small number of its inhabitants.

F I N I S.

BIBLIOLIFE

Old Books Deserve a New Life
www.bibliolife.com

Did you know that you can get most of our titles in our trademark **EasyScript**™ print format? **EasyScript**™ provides readers with a larger than average typeface, for a reading experience that's easier on the eyes.

Did you know that we have an ever-growing collection of books in many languages?

Order online:
www.bibliolife.com/store

Or to exclusively browse our **EasyScript**™ collection:
www.bibliogrande.com

At BiblioLife, we aim to make knowledge more accessible by making thousands of titles available to you – quickly and affordably.

Contact us:
BiblioLife
PO Box 21206
Charleston, SC 29413

LaVergne, TN USA
04 January 2011
210982LV00003B/79/P